Ruth

Growth unto Maturity

Titus Chu

Ruth: Growth unto Maturity
by Titus Chu

First Edition: April 2004
Second Edition: April 2010
Third Edition: August 2013
PDF & Print on Demand

Distributed by
The Church in Cleveland Literature Service
3150 Warren Road
Cleveland, Ohio 44111

Available for purchase online.
Printed by CreateSpace,
an Amazon.com company.

Download the PDF version of this book at
www.MinistryMessages.org

Please send correspondence by email to
TheEditors@MinistryMessages.org

Published by
Good Land Publishers
Ann Arbor, Michigan

Contents

1. Freshness after Failure, Famine, and Death   3
   Ruth 1:1–1:5

2. The Path to a Real Christ   9
   Ruth 1:6

3. Returning to the Riches in God's House   17
   Ruth 1:6–1:21

4. Finding Resurrection in the Lord's Field   27
   Ruth 1:22–2:3

5. Christ's Care in the Church Life   37
   Ruth 2:3–2:23

6. Finding Christ under God's Arrangement   49
   Ruth 3:1–3:13

7. Preparation in the Night   61
   Ruth 3:1–3:18

8. Brought into Union with Christ   71
   Ruth 4:1–4:18

   Works Cited   85

This book consists of messages given by Titus Chu in Montreal, Canada, to college students from around the Great Lakes in August 2003. These messages focus upon our growth and progress in the church life, which, as we are under the shepherding of life and the operation of the Lord's death and resurrection, will ultimately result in that complete union with Christ for which we long. Praise Him for being such a Savior! How we yearn for the day we will be able to say that He and we are one forever, and that nothing is left to compete with Him in our hearts.

> *"...I press on, that I may lay hold of that for which Christ Jesus has also laid hold of me."*
>
> *—Philippians 3:12*

The editors

1

Freshness after
Failure, Famine, and Death

How good it is to come to God's Word! The purpose of this study is to gain a deeper enjoyment of life, a deeper understanding of truth, and a further perfecting of our service in the church life.

The Place of Ruth in the Bible

What part does the book of Ruth play in the Bible? It provides a marvelous, spiritual wash basin! It follows the book of Judges, which is an extremely messy book. As we read the Bible beginning from Genesis, we run into all kinds of discouraging and depressing things. Eventually, when we come to Judges, we find that everything among God's people is in a very poor situation. Even the judges raised up by God to rescue His people do not appear to be the best patterns to follow. Samson had little with which to commend himself. For instance, in his dying prayer he prays *he* would be avenged, not that God would gain anything (Judg. 16:28). Gideon allowed a worship center to be set up outside of Jerusalem (Judg. 8:22–27). Deborah claims she will come under the authority of Barak yet acts in a way that is not properly related to him (Judg. 4). The book of Judges is full of impurity—idolatry, immorality, brutality, rebellion, and failure.

Following Judges, however, we find that God has prepared a wonderful "bath" filled with sweet, spiritual water. Out from the midst of all that failure, God is able to gain something so sweet and pure for Himself. It seems no other book in the Bible can compare to Ruth in purity.

The book of Ruth reveals that overcomers can be produced in any situation, regardless how poor it may seem. Its events take place during the reign of the judges, a time when the leadership in Israel was "out of order." Yet from the midst of such an abnormal situation emerges an old woman named Naomi, a young woman named Ruth, and a righteous man named Boaz. The book of Ruth focuses on these three persons.

Outwardly, the story in Ruth begins on a discouraging note. Due to famine, a man, his wife (Naomi), and their two sons leave the good land and go to Moab, a land of curse. The two sons marry Moabite women but soon die, as does Naomi's husband, leaving three widows. Though this is tragic, if Naomi had never gone to Moab, Ruth, one of her daughters-in-law, would never have found her way into the good land. Boaz, the man needed to complete this story, awaited her in Israel.

The people of Moab were related to God's people, for they were descendants of Abraham's nephew Lot. They knew Jehovah, but their origin was through the terrible sin of incest between Lot and one of his daughters (Gen. 19:30–38). The incident of Judah with his daughter-in-law Tamar (Gen. 38) is another such story alluded to in this pure book of Ruth (4:12). The Bible tells us about things just as they happened. It does not mince words. It includes these terrible stories to show us how merciful God is and to show us something quite marvelous. If such stories were not in the Bible, there could be no Ruth. The Lord Jesus Himself eventually came forth from this situation, for Ruth was His ancestor.

Facing Famine in the House of Bread

The book of Ruth begins by giving us this background: "Now in the days when the judges ruled, there was a famine in the land. And a man from Bethlehem in Judah went down to dwell as a sojourner in the country of Moab, he and his wife and his two sons" (1:1). This is something that took place in the days of the judges, but it is as true today as it was then. When the leadership has problems, God's people experience famine. Bethlehem means "house of bread" (Brown). This family was in a place where they should have enjoyed an abundance of food, but instead they experienced famine!

This man of Bethlehem changed his place of dwelling. He had been living in God's good land of promise in the House of Bread. At some point, however, he became a sojourner in the land of Moab and was no longer in his homeland.

Elimelech, Naomi, and Their Two Sons

This Bethlehemite's name was Elimelech, which means "my God is King" (Brown). How could a man with such a name end up in the land of Moab? Simply because the leaders of God's people did not do a good job. A man with the name "My God Is King", dwelling in the good land in a city named "House of Bread", departed to sojourn in a place that was under God's curse, all because the leaders didn't know how to lead.

Elimelech's wife was named Naomi, which means "pleasant" (Strong). Surely anyone attached to a person named "My God Is King" would become a pleasant person! This wonderfully-named couple produced two sons. One was named Mahlon, and the other was named Chilion.

Mahlon means "mild" (Young). Many who have consecrated themselves strongly to the Lord have children who seem quite mild in comparison.

The second son's name was Chilion, which means "pining away" (Brown) or "wasting away" (Davis). What is the reason you attend Christian conferences? Why do you read the Bible? Why do you behave in a certain way? Is it because others expect you to? This is often the situation among children raised in Christian families: either they are "mild" or they are "pining away."

As represented by their names, Elimelech and Naomi seem to have been an admirable couple. The husband was consecrated, and the wife experienced blessing due to his stand. One day, however, they encountered famine in the "House of Bread."

Experiencing Famine and Wandering in the Church Life

I believe all who love the Lord eventually experience this discrepancy, encountering famine in the "House of Bread." They begin to wonder, "What am I doing here? Look at those around me—this one is peculiar, and that one is no help. The situation in the church is intolerable." They lose their ability to receive nourishment and thus experience hunger in the church life. They begin looking around for a more favorable environment for themselves.

What should Elimelech have done when there was no bread? That was the time to trust the Lord. He should have said, "God is still my King. I trust in Him. Judges come and judges go, but my Lord remains the same." Instead, he and his wife left the land of promise and sojourned in the land of Moab to see if they could find food there. If there seems to be a famine in the church life, remember this: the church is still the church, and the Lord is still the Lord.

Elimelech Dying in Moab

Eventually this good man, Elimelech, died. Spiritually, there can be no other result when we depart from the place of food. Once we begin to partake of the riches of the world, we are led further and further from the Lord's supply. For instance, if we are interested in getting a degree in management, we eventually feel that our degree must be an MBA. And if we are to get an MBA, it must be from a prestigious institution such as Harvard. And once we have that prestigious MBA, we must get a good job.

Then, after we find a good job, we are not satisfied until we are the CEO. After we are the CEO, we still will not be satisfied— simply because we do not yet possess the whole world! The world is attractive, and no matter how much we are told that it is of the Devil, we still find it attractive. No matter how many times we read the verse, "Love not the world," we still feel that driving a Lexus is more enjoyable than driving a Toyota.

As a student I attended Taiwan University, the top university in Taiwan. Many of my classmates earned Ph.D.'s and pursued what the world had to offer. Many of them became leaders in various fields. I recently heard that one of my classmates spoke to a number of the others about the Lord, and many were receptive. Now that they are old, most of them probably realize that, although they attained what they desired from the world, nothing remains for them but death. Without the Lord, all die.

Marrying Moabite Women

Naomi's two sons married Moabite women. Chilion married a woman named Orpah, which means "youthful freshness" (Young), and Mahlon married a woman named Ruth, which comes from a root word meaning "companion" or "shepherd" (Strong). After marrying Moabite women, Naomi's two sons died. This was of great consequence. In order to be considered a Jew, one must have a Jewish mother. Any descendants of these sons could not have been counted among God's people. Descendants of Moab were barred from entering into the Lord's congregation for ten generations (Deut. 23:3).

This is true spiritually. If we become married to our job, we are finished as far as God's purpose is concerned. To have a job is one thing, but to become married to it is another. We should take a proper job unless the Lord leads us to serve Him full-time, but we should not become married to our job, regardless of its status or pay.

How surprising! After sojourning in the land of Moab, the son named "Pining Away" (Chilion) married someone named

"Youthful Freshness" (Orpah), and the son named "Mild" (Mahlon) married an even better person named "Intimate Companion," or "Shepherd" (Ruth). This is a marvelous picture. When we are so weak and discouraged, the Lord does something for Himself. We may meet rejection and experience discouragement after being so optimistic about our efforts in the gospel. As we continue to speak to others in this weak and withered condition, suddenly someone responds. Perhaps this person is a believer who is very fresh. And then another responds who becomes our companion and even shepherds us.

Losing yet Gaining

The Lord uses every situation. He used the messy situation under the judges and the famine. He used the weakness of Elimelech in leading his family out of God's promised land into the land of the Moabites. Eventually all these things pass away, and the Lord gains another generation, taking a further step toward what He desires. Through these events, the Lord brought Ruth out of the land of Moab into the land of His people.

After we have lost "My God Is King" (Elimelech), "Mildness" (Mahlon), and "Pining Away" (Chilion), we need a new beginning. This is brought in with "Freshness" (Orpah). Although freshness is needed at the beginning, it will prove insufficient to carry us through. We also need "Intimate Companion" or "Shepherd" (Ruth). Naomi found that this life-relationship, represented by Ruth, became her supporting strength. Now, in the reality of intimate companionship, we are ready to return to Bethlehem.

2

The Path to a Real Christ

The names in the Old Testament are very meaningful. As we have seen, a man named "My God Is King" (Elimelech) married a woman named "Pleasant" (Naomi) and had two sons, "Mild" (Mahlon) and "Pining Away" (Chilion). This family left the "House of Bread" (Bethlehem) in the good land to journey to the land of the Moabites, a people cursed by God.

They left the good land because of famine. There was a shortage of food in the "House of Bread." This took place during the rule of the judges, a time of confusion and inadequate leadership. Inadequate leadership results in an inadequate supply of food among God's people.

Inadequate Leadership Responsible for Famine

The judges of that day had more authority than any President of the United States. In America, there are checks and balances built into the government. In Israel at that time, the judge held absolute power to muster the people for war and to make and enforce laws and policy. We should realize, however, that it is a person's constitution that determines the nature of his leadership. If a church's elders are healthy, that church will be healthy. If the elders pray, that church will pray. How the elders exercise determines how the believers in that local church will exercise. The Lord's move on the earth is carried out through ministries, not positions. How a person is constituted determines how he will exercise leadership.

It seems that not one of the judges who ruled up to the time of Ruth knew the Lord properly. Instead, there was a great lack in leadership, and this translated into a lack of nourishment for God's people. So Elimelech, his wife Naomi, and their two sons Mahlon and Chilion left to sojourn in the land of Moab.

In this land of cursed people, son "Pining Away" married a woman named "Fresh," and son "Mild" married a woman named "Intimate Companion" (or "Shepherd"). Eventually, there was a return to the good land, and something was produced for God. Thus, in order to reach the point where something could be produced for God, three stages of experience are necessary.

Stage One: A Wonderful Church Life

The first level of experience is that of Bethlehem where Elimelech and Naomi experienced the bountiful riches in the good land, the place of divine blessings. If we have never experienced this first stage in our Christian life, we cannot become a lover of Christ and the church. In this first stage, we see how wonderful the Christian life and the church life are. We are captured and can declare, "My God is King!" Pleasantness accompanies us.

To those in this stage, the church life is full of food. They are in love with the church life, and they love the brothers and sisters. In their experience, the Lord is so rich. They can sing with appreciation, "Glorious church life—feasting from such a rich store!"

Stage Two: Spiritual Famine

Eventually we enter another stage. After a period of time, we may comment, "The leaders could have done this instead of that," or, "Things are different; they are not as rich as before." Perhaps things really are not as rich as before, or they may just seem less rich because our opinions have turned our hearts away from Christ. It is inevitable that in a rich church life people will eventually feel things are not as wonderful as they once were, that something is short. When this happens, we begin to have thoughts about other things. This is the onset of famine. Such an experience may affect just one individual or an entire church. However, everyone who has been caught by the Lord will encounter this feeling and perceive a lack.

When a church enters into this experience, its members will begin to look elsewhere for nourishment. Some may seek out the blessings they hear other groups are experiencing. They may leave to join other congregations or to start their own Christian group. Some will start wandering, seeking out help from a variety of other sources.

When churches or individuals experience such a famine, the Lord is still with them. If some begin to complain about or question the church's leadership, however, we need to learn that this is dangerous territory. Don't get involved with rebellion. Don't get involved with any so-called fellowship with the intent of undermining the leadership, no matter how things may seem. Learn to say, "I don't want to be involved." It is a great protection to your Christian life to avoid any and all such talk.

A famine is a time of testing. Previously, everyone experienced an abundance of food. Now, food is not so easy to come by. When confronting such times of famine, we should be happy because these are the times when we learn to appreciate what the Lord provides.

In my early years, my family was relatively wealthy, for my father held a high rank in the military. We had household servants who cooked for us and took care of our needs. When we walked to school, we could afford little charcoal hand-warmers that the other students envied. This was our situation until we had to flee from the Communists, who were taking over China. At that time we had very little to eat, and we had to move quickly from place to place. As children, however, we actually treasured these times more than those when we had much, because our parents were with us, and we saw how they struggled to take care of our needs. This was a happy time for us. That experience prepared me for all that would happen later in my life. If it were not for those four or five years of hardship, I do not believe I would know how to handle things today. Spiritually, it is the same.

In this stage of famine, we become failures in the Christian life. We either end up falling more and more into things of the world, such as entertainment, or we occupy ourselves with things other than the church life. Some may seek fulfillment in the world instead of remaining fully in the church life. We shouldn't judge them. They may be weak, but this is a part of the process of growth. In the beginning, we claimed we would follow the Lord to the end. When we come to this stage, however, we have to confess that we are just too weak to go on.

When the Lord asked His disciples if they were able to be baptized with the baptism He was baptized with, they claimed they were able (Matt. 20:22; cf. 26:35). How many were actually able to follow Him all the way to the cross? Not one! Whatever degree we are able to follow the Lord is due to His mercy. Everyone who loves the Lord and experiences His blessing will eventually also experience dryness and limitation. Those in this situation realize that the only reason they can still love the Lord is because of His grace. Such Christians begin to experience something real in their relationship with the Lord; they no longer live in dreams.

We should not be so quick to judge others as being good or bad. All who follow the Lord will experience many things on their lifelong journey. Their success or failure will not be determined until their last breath. Everything beforehand is a part of the process. Whether at a certain moment we are prevailing, or whether at a certain moment we are weak, for sure, we will pass from the joyful initial stage to the stage of dissatisfaction and seeming failure. The Lord allows us to experience each of these stages so that we may really know Him.

At this time the focus in the book of Ruth turns from the men to Naomi, a woman. Her husband and her two sons have all died. Naomi's children represented her hope, and her husband was the person she relied upon. Now Naomi had no hope and nothing left to rely upon.

In our church life, or in our Christian life, we often rely upon or set our hope on something other than the Lord Himself. Perhaps it is our spiritual ability or our serving in the church life. The Lord eventually must take these things away. This is a very deep lesson. Perhaps we really love serving the young people and feel that without serving them our Christian life would have no hope. Or we may feel that we can rely upon our spiritual parents in the church life. The Lord will eventually bring us to the point that we can no longer rely upon such things. Eventually, the only person who can be our hope and supply is the Lord Himself.

Paul said that he planted and that Apollos watered, but only God Himself could give the increase or growth (1 Cor. 3:6). This is a lesson even those young in the Lord can experience. We should go to fellow believers for fellowship, but we should not rely upon them more than we rely upon the Lord Himself. Others can help us to read the Bible, pray, or understand certain things, but they cannot give us growth. Only the Lord Himself can do this.

The Lord brought Naomi to such an experience. Both her husband and her two sons were taken from her, and she was left alone. There was nothing left for her to rely upon or to hope in, yet this was when she experienced a spiritual revival.

Stage Three: Returning to Christ Alone

To whom is the Lord more precious—to those who have no failure, or to those who experience the Lord in their failure and weakness? Surely those who come to know their weakness and shortcomings can know the Lord in a deeper way. For this to happen, however, we must come to the Lord in our weakness.

When I was in the military, I used every spare moment to read the Bible. Then I prayed a bold prayer: "Lord, You cannot ask me to do better than this. Every minute, every break, and every opportunity I am reading Your Word. Every morning I am in Your presence. Thank You, Lord, that I love You so much." I should have prayed, "Lord, draw me to Yourself even more."

That same day, I experienced a severe chest pain and went to lie down. The next day I went to the base hospital. I was X-rayed and the image was sent out for analysis. On the Lord's Day, I conducted the singing as usual in the children's meeting, coughing all the while. That Monday I received a letter by express delivery instructing me to go to the hospital immediately. My lung had collapsed. I was in the hospital for four weeks recuperating. During that time I could not read the Bible at all, yet the Lord became so rich to me.

Many times we tell the Lord that we are doing something for Him or that we are so much for Him. All the Lord has to do is to touch us a little, and then we find we can do nothing for Him. He just touched my lung a little, and I had no strength even to read the Bible. The Lord desires that we cling to Him more than to anything else, even more than studying the Bible, giving messages, or preaching the gospel. Of course, when we have the Lord, we will do many of these things. What becomes most precious to us is not any of these outward things but Christ Himself.

It is during the hard times that Christ becomes most real to us. When we are in difficulties, we pursue Christ more desperately. Naomi's loss of her husband and two sons surely brought her into a deep valley. Yet after all her suffering, she rose up and became a spiritual woman.

She arose, along with her daughters-in-law, and sought to return to Israel, for she had heard that the Lord had visited His people and had supplied them with bread. She now realized that everything the world had to offer amounted to nothing, and she was ready to return.

A very wealthy man told me not long ago that what Solomon said is really true—everything under the sun *is* vanity (Eccl. 1:2–3). His wealth was extraordinary, yet his realization was, "Vanity of vanities." Many of my schoolmates were very ambitious when they were in college. They planned to become ambassadors, CEOs, or professors. At a recent class reunion some of them said that they wished they had chosen the path I chose. Why are so many of them open to the gospel right now, at this late stage in their lives? It is because they have discovered that nothing they have pursued is of any value. They envy me, for they know that I have found the storehouse of food. Yet they do not know the half of it. They do not know how I have enjoyed and gained Christ in the past fifty years, and how rich He has become to me. Christ has been wrought into me and has become my focus, my portion, and my operation.

The Lord has visited His people and has given them food. The real satisfaction is with Christ Himself. When some see this, they rise up, realizing that only Christ is worth pursuing. May the Lord have mercy upon us that we may simply pursue Christ!

3

Returning to the Riches in God's House

As we grow to Christian maturity, we will experience three things: we will taste Christ's riches (Bethlehem), then we will confront dryness either individually or corporately (famine), and finally, we will experience a return to the Supplier of the riches.

The reason we love the Lord is because He is so lovely (1 John 4:19). If we have never been drawn by the Lord, our love for Him will be hollow. We should experience the riches of the Lord in many aspects—the more the better. When we enjoy Him in this way, we are captured by Him. Those who have known the Lord and His riches can never forget Him, but if we abide in the riches alone, we may never come to know the Supplier of the rich enjoyment, for the riches we enjoy may replace the Lord Himself.

Therefore, the Lord allows each of us to experience a dryness in our church life or in our personal Christian life. Eventually the Lord will bring us into an experience of famine. Everyone in the church life may feel that something is insufficient and that the Lord's presence is no longer so sustaining, or only some individuals among them may feel so.

When we experience the Lord's daily supply of riches, we tend to forget about Him. We do not fully appreciate what we are enjoying. Famine exposes who we are and where we are. When we have plenty of food, we are able to boast, "My God is King" (Elimelech), but how do we react when the food supply dries up? Do we cling more closely to the Lord, or do we seek to meet our needs elsewhere?

Elimelech had a meaningful name, but when famine came, it

turned out to be a mere slogan. God did not remain his King. This is why Elimelech had to die in Moab. When what we have is merely a slogan, it cannot match God. It must be exposed and allowed to die. By such a death, the Lord produces something for Himself. Hopefully this process will not take too long.

Returning to Bethlehem for the Lord Himself

Sometimes we hear that some who departed from the church life have returned after many years. On the one hand, we are happy to hear this, for they have returned to the "House of Bread." On the other hand, we feel sad about the time that was wasted. We must learn from this not to depart when we confront weakness, depression, or hardship. We must learn to turn to the Lord. He is *always* available.

After feasting and enjoying comes famine, exposure, and death. Following this, the book of Ruth tells us that Naomi rose up with her two daughters-in-law in order to return from the country of Moab, for she had heard that the Lord had visited His people by giving them bread (Ruth 1:6). Perhaps we think Naomi returned primarily for food, but according to the word here, it was because she heard that "the Lord had visited His people." Her interest was no longer just the riches of the Lord; it was now the Lord Himself.

During our first years in the church life, we fell in love with the revelations, the meetings, the sweetness among the believers, and the atmosphere of blessedness. In spite of all these enjoyable experiences, eventually we find we are unable to fully put our trust in the One who provides them. Therefore, when any of these precious experiences dry up, we immediately take off on a sojourn. We remove ourselves from the Lord and His people and in the process find out who we really are. We are not the great believers we thought we were. After we are touched by the Lord about our relying upon other things, we are finally able to come to Him as we should. Now the focus is no longer on the food, but on the Lord Himself. Needless to say, where the Lord is, there will be food.

This is the journey of every believer who seeks the Lord. When we come to this stage, our heart returns to Bethlehem, for that is where the Lord is. Our heart desires the Lord and focuses on Him, not on the blessings He provides. Therefore, we rise up to go to where we hear He is, and we re-consecrate ourselves to Him.

Returning with a Selfless Humanity That Matches the Lord

Consider Naomi and how she speaks after the death of her husband and two sons. Through her words we see she is a spiritual person in a very human way. Naomi has only her two daughters-in-law left to her. If they leave, she will be totally alone, yet she trusts in the Lord for herself. She considers the need of her daughters-in-law and encourages them to go back to their mothers' homes. Likewise, we must be spiritual to the point that we have a high humanity, the humanity of Jesus.

Naomi's word reveals her reliance upon the Lord. She tells these two women, "The Lord deal kindly with you…" (Ruth 1:8). She has experienced the Lord's discipline to the point that she has lost everything, but as one who has lost everything, she has really begun to know the Lord. She realizes that her daughters-in-law would have no way to follow God in their homeland. She cannot say, "May you grow to maturity here in Moab." But still she says, "The Lord deal kindly with you, as you have dealt with the dead and with me." This verse reveals something so sincere and selfless. She advises them to remarry, for she has no way to provide them with husbands. Even as her heart aches, remembering her sons, she tells them to find other husbands. Then they kiss and embrace and weep together. What a touching sight— three widows weeping together, preparing to go their separate ways alone.

When the two younger widows said that they would go with her, Naomi said, "Turn back, my daughters; why will you go with me? Are there still sons in my womb, that they may be your husbands? Turn back, my daughters, go—for I am too old to have a husband. If I should say I have hope, if I should have a husband tonight and should also bear sons, would you wait for them till they were grown?" (Ruth 1:11–13). According to the Old Testament, the brother of a dead husband was to take his brother's wife as his own in order to raise up children in his brother's name (Deut. 25:5). Naomi was past childbearing age, and even if she were able to marry and give birth, could Orpah and Ruth wait until her children had grown old enough for marriage? Of course not. This is what Naomi was saying here. Furthermore, they were foreigners to Israel and would be treated as such in Israel. What would Orpah and Ruth's future be if they were to return to Israel with Naomi? Therefore Naomi counseled them to return to their families, even though it meant Naomi would be left on her own.

Again Naomi mentions the Lord: "It grieves me very much for your sakes that the hand of the Lord has gone out against me" (Ruth 1:13). Noami recognizes that the Lord's dealing hand has been against her. Her family has left Bethlehem, and she has suffered the loss of her husband and her sons. She has experienced the Lord's hand of discipline, yet she does not display any bitterness toward the Lord. She does not say, "The Lord in His severity has pushed me beyond the limits of my endurance and has struck me down." Those who say such things do not know the Lord. After many years of the Lord's dealings, Naomi's humanity manifests something very spiritual. She places the needs of her daughters-in-law above her own.

Expressing Spirituality through a High Humanity

Naomi recognized the Lord's hand in all that happened to her. She also exercised a genuine concern for others and exhibited a high humanity. We should have such a heart, always seeking the good of others. If a brother is weak, we should consider how we might strengthen him. If a sister is cold toward the Lord, we should struggle to find a way to help her love the Lord. If we simply judge others and place demands upon them, this indicates a lack in our humanity. We should learn of Naomi, for even in her distress she cared for the needs of others more than for her own needs. She was mature enough that she could consider others in such a way, entrusting herself and them to the Lord.

If we do not know how to live such a selfless life, we can never be spiritual. Those who are truly spiritual possess a high humanity. Our spirituality is expressed through our humanity. Sometimes instead of being merciful, we are judgmental toward others. Consider the story in *Les Misérables*. After Valjean stole from the priest who had taken him in and fed him, some might feel that the priest should have told the arresting officer, "Throw that ungrateful thief into jail!" Instead he said, "No, these things are gifts from me to him. Here, you forgot the other silver candlestick. Take that as well." That human act brought about the repentance of Valjean. That example has merit. Higher spirituality is expressed through higher humanity. Apart from a proper humanity, we should not even talk about being spiritual.

Companionship and Shepherding

Orpah kissed her mother-in-law, which meant she was taking Naomi's advice and leaving, whereas Ruth clung to Naomi. Since Orpah means "youthful freshness" and Ruth's name refers to companionship and shepherding, it would seem that freshness does not mean as much to God as shepherding. Comparatively speaking, our divine exercise of shepherding is of more value to God than our condition of freshness.

Naomi advised Ruth again to return with her sister-in-law, but Ruth was adamant. Why would Naomi allow Ruth to return with her, knowing how much suffering Ruth would face as an accursed foreigner? Regardless of the reason, it certainly was a comfort to Naomi to have Ruth accompany her. Ruth said, "Entreat me not to leave you, or to turn back from following after you; for wherever you go, I will go; and wherever you lodge, I will lodge; your people shall be my people, and your God, my God. Where you die, I will die, and there will I be buried. The Lord do so to me, and more also, if anything but death parts you and me" (Ruth 1:16–17).

Following Those Who Are More Mature

I hope the young people among us could have a heart to say such a thing to an older one. I'm afraid quite often the opposite is the case. Most young people distance themselves from those who are older, as much as possible. Instead of saying, "Entreat me not to leave you," they would say, "Please leave and don't bother me anymore." If we want to follow the Lord and grow properly, we need to attach ourselves to someone like Naomi. Those who are younger have to recognize that some among them are more mature in the Lord and that the older ones' God needs to become their God. If this is their realization, there is good reason to have hope for the younger generation.

When I was first saved, I had such an older one. I observed him and followed him. I learned much from that brother, including how to groan before the Lord. Later, when I went to another district in Taipei, I contacted the leading brother there and told him, "I am moving here, and I need to be under someone and to learn from someone. I'd like to place myself under you." He must have been happy to see such a young man drop out of the heavens like that. I learned much from him as well. He had an effective way of working with children, and I benefited. I made use of his way of working with children when I went to other places. To others this brother may not have been so noteworthy, but I received a lot of help from him. Learn to follow and receive help from older ones with whom the Lord places you. We should also realize that it is not practical to follow someone who lives far away from us. We all need someone we can follow. My observation is that those who refuse to do so will struggle spiritually and may even become a source of difficulty.

To be in the church life without someone to follow is to be a wanderer. It does not matter how poor your church appears to be; I can guarantee you that it has at least one person who is ahead of you spiritually. The young people in particular have to learn to attach themselves to believers who are more mature in the Lord.

This is how Ruth began following the Lord—by following an older sister. Why did she choose to follow Naomi? It was because of Naomi's firm faith in God and because of the high humanity she exhibited. How decisive Ruth's declaration was! She trusted in Naomi's God to accomplish her desire and to carry out her vow. Apart from Naomi, Ruth could never have made such a consecration. It was Naomi's experience in the Lord that made it possible for Ruth to follow Him in the same manner. The God of Naomi attracted Ruth both through Naomi's humanity and because of the evidence of His faithful hand upon her.

Spiritual Parents in the Church Life

I hope that there are many mature believers like Naomi among us. We need parents more than we need teachers (1 Cor. 4:15). Teachers are those who give you a lesson and, having done their job, can go to sleep. Parents, however, don't sleep so easily because they want to care for their children beyond their ability or means. We should ask the Lord to give us such parents in the church life. Parents are always anxious to see their children grow well. Such parental involvement results in headaches for both parent and child. The main point is this: in the church life we should not be alone. We should have someone caring for us, and we should also care for someone.

Experiencing the All-sufficient One through Hardship

After Ruth had made her decision, Naomi stopped trying to

dissuade her, and they returned to Bethlehem together. What a homecoming! They had finally returned to the storehouse of food. The whole city was stirred by Naomi's return (Ruth 1:19). Some of the women said, "Is this Naomi?" Perhaps they could not believe this acquaintance from years ago could be so changed by age and hardship. To this she replied, "Do not call me Naomi [pleasant]. Call me Mara [bitter], for the Almighty has dealt very bitterly with me. I went out full, and the Lord has brought me home again empty. Why do you call me Naomi, since the Lord has testified against me, and the Almighty has afflicted me?" (Ruth 1:20–21). This is a further sign of her maturity. She realized that she no longer possessed anything. All that she formerly had, she had lost. Because of this, she no longer trusted in herself. Not only did she manifest a high humanity and proclaim Jehovah, but she also had a deep realization that she had nothing in which to boast.

Her testimony was that God was the All-sufficient One (*Shaddai* in Ruth 1:20–21; although it is rendered "Almighty," the Hebrew word emphasizes that He is a God who richly supplies). Everything else that she had leaned upon and hoped in had been stripped away, but God had been faithful to supply her. She had no fortune, nor any portion in the good land. All she had was a woman of a cursed people accompanying her. Her testimony was that her situation was no longer pleasant but bitter. Yet if you had asked further, she would have continued by saying, "The Lord has been faithful." Her situation seemed hopeless, yet her realization was that God was the All-sufficient One.

Sometimes we do not understand how God supplies us, yet we realize that we have been supplied. Outwardly, it seems we have been losing instead of gaining. Yet inwardly we realize that we have gained something in the midst of all our loss. It has not been a smooth or pleasant way, and we are keenly aware of what has been taken from us. However, in this condition we can testify that the Lord really is the All-sufficient One. He is not only the Almighty One who is able to do great things for us, but He is also all-sufficient in what He Himself has become to us. We went out full and now come back empty, but in all this the Lord has proven Himself to us, and He Himself has become our possession.

I believe that those who achieve something in the world can be filled with accomplishments and other things, but they cannot know God as their All-sufficient One. When they achieve some success, they may experience a certain kind of satisfaction, even of being filled. But after many years, I believe that all this is exposed as being empty. After forty years at a company, retiring employees are sent away with a party and a gold watch. They come into the company full of ambition and expectation, and they leave empty, especially if they do not have the Lord. Yet Naomi said, "I went out full, and the Lord has brought me home again empty. Why do you call me Naomi, since the Lord has testified against me, and the All-Sufficient One has afflicted me?" (Ruth 1:21, Heb.). Because God is the All-sufficient One, He provides for you as He disciplines and takes from you. His dealings may seem harsh in what He gives and takes away, but He Himself will become your supply in the process.

4

Finding Resurrection in the Lord's Field

The first chapter of Ruth concludes with Naomi and Ruth returning to Bethlehem from the land of Moab "at the beginning of barley harvest" (v. 22). Their intention was to return to God's provision (v. 6). After all her tragic experience in the land of Moab, Naomi became sensitive to God Himself and to His activity. Before this time, Bethlehem was a storehouse of food in name only. Now, however, Bethlehem is a place the Lord Himself has visited by giving His people bread (v. 6). Naomi's previous experience in Bethlehem was one of famine and the lack of the Lord's blessing. Now she hears about the Lord's blessing in Bethlehem and realizes that when she has the Lord, she has food, and if she is short of food, she is short of the Lord Himself. In the Lord's absence, food may or may not be there, but when we have the Lord's presence, we assuredly also have the Lord's supply.

Returning for Food and Finding a Feast

Ruth and Naomi thus returned with the intention of finding God and finding food. What they actually found when they returned, however, was a feast, a celebration. It was more than simply finding food; it was the beginning of barley harvest. Today, those who have experienced spiritual famine and return to the church life find something far beyond their expectation. They are seeking food, but instead they find a feast! They do not anticipate that the Christ they are coming to partake of is such a bountiful Christ.

Boaz: A Relative with a Rich Supply

With all this as the background, chapter two begins, "There was a relative of Naomi's husband, a man of great wealth, of the family of Elimelech. His name was Boaz." In other words, Boaz was a man of rich supply. He was related to "My God Is King" (Elimelech), but his own name means "in him is strength" (Davis). This same name was given to one of the two pillars that upheld the temple of the Lord (1 Kings 7:21). Boaz was very rich and able to meet any need a person might have.

Perhaps we feel that we are too weak to partake of all the riches of Christ, who is our Boaz. When we come to God's house, however, we find that this One even has the ability to supply us with what is needed to partake of His riches. He can supply us whether we are strong or weak. Whatever we need, He is. Our Lord's unsearchable riches become our supply. Regardless of our state, in Him is strength. Even if we are spiritually sick and too weak to eat, we have a Boaz who can take care of us, for in Him is strength. He is so unsearchably rich.

A Testimony of Learning to Know Christ as Boaz

In my fifty years' experience of following the Lord, He has never come up short. I am continually amazed at Him. We cannot exhaust His riches. We have a song that says, "The half cannot be fancied of such a treasure store, and every day He's dearer than He ever was before." Many strive diligently for years in a particular area and eventually become experts, but as to Christ, we can never say that we have done more than scratch the surface. Even though I have been pursuing the Lord for half a century, I still feel I have only entered the gate. The Lord has riches prepared for us that we will be receiving and appreciating throughout all eternity.

I am amazed that, after all I have encountered throughout my life, I am still pursuing Christ. When I first began following the Lord in high school, I had many experiences in which Christ's supply became so real to me. After I graduated, I did not think I could get into National Taiwan University, the best university in Taiwan, so I asked the Lord if He would allow me to get into a teachers college. This He did, but I ended up in the department that trained Boy Scout instructors—at that time, entrance into every university and even every department was dependent upon one's score on the post-high-school exam. I asked Him why, and He told me, "You never told Me which department you wanted. I answered your prayer."

I felt this was an insufficient answer to my prayer since this department did not even grant a two-year degree. Therefore I took the examination again a year later and scored high enough to enter a regular university. When I arrived at the admissions office, however, they claimed I had falsified the document. I was so angry! I did not feel I should give up easily, so I asked my father to help. He put on his general's uniform, went down to the office, and demanded action. They admitted their error, but by the time they did, half the school year was over, and nothing could be done.

The third time, I took the test with my younger brother. We knew someone who worked in the testing bureau who could let us know the results a day earlier than everyone else. We waited by the phone at the prescribed hour, and when the phone rang, I was the one to pick it up. The caller said, "Congratulations to your brother! He got into Taiwan University." I asked him, "How about me?" He said, "You were one point short of placement at Taiwan University."

I cannot tell you my feeling at that moment. I realized that this was the Lord's doing. After I congratulated my brother, my mother asked, "How about you?" I told her, and she said, "I wish it were you, and not your brother, who got into Taiwan University." Because of my mother's disappointment over me, instead of holding a celebration for my brother, the family mourned my failure. My brother and I were the only two smiling, but he could not do so publicly for my sake. To me at that moment, however, the Lord was so real.

Eventually, I got into Taiwan University, but not through the standard entrance exam. I got in through a side door, transferring from the university at which I had been placed. I passed through a lot of frustrating things before I graduated from Taiwan University. Through all these situations I discovered how rich the Lord is. It seemed that others were more blessed outwardly, but through these outwardly distressing situations, my Lord proved Himself to me. I have to say that He is really my Boaz—"in Him is strength." His way was different from my way, and His plan was much higher than mine. What happened to me? I found Boaz.

Knowing Christ as my Boaz became my strength to stand in later years. I first came to the United States on a student visa, but once I arrived my plans changed. I went to the immigration office to get my visa changed so that I could work here. The man at the desk looked miserable. I asked him about changing my status, and he told me it would be impossible. It seemed that the Lord had brought me to the United States for twenty days only to send me back so soon. As the man walked out of the room, however, his supervisor came in and asked what was going on. When he told him, for some reason his supervisor said, "What's wrong with that? Give him the permit." I had to marvel. In twenty seconds, the Lord had reversed my situation and allowed me to stay. I had to praise the Lord for His trustworthiness. If instead, I had argued, "But you can't send me back!" how could I stand before the Lord as I do today? I simply received that situation from the Lord, believing that whatever happened would be best for me. When we begin to follow the Lord, we have no idea how rich the Lord will be to us.

Christ Our Supply and Strength

The Lord's riches are beyond our understanding. If we need health, He can give us health. If we need strength, He can supply strength. Whatever we ask, He is wealthy enough to provide because He is the All-sufficient One. Don't depend upon your income, your family, or even yourself. At some point, everything and everyone we depend upon will fail. For all the things needed in our lives, we must learn to trust in the Lord. He will never go bankrupt. He will never come up short. He will even become the strength we need to follow Him. Such a Christ is related to us.

Not only was Boaz a man of wealth, but his name means "in him is strength." In my fifty years of following the Lord, nothing has been easy. Recently I told my wife, "As I consider these fifty years...," and I stopped; tears came to my eyes. I had a lot of feeling toward the Lord whom I served. It was as if I were telling Him, "Lord, had I known it would be this hard, I might not have followed You." My wife was surprised by my tears. She put her arm around me and said, "All is well." Why am I still here serving the Lord? I feel that if the Lord would give me twenty more years to live, I would give them all to Him. My desire is that in each remaining year I might be more and more productive, of more value, and more of a blessing to the body of Christ. Why is this? It is because Christ is my Boaz; "in Him is strength." We are limited and fragile people. The Lord would encourage us, knowing that things sometimes are too hard to bear. He reminds us that He is our High Priest who sympathizes with our weaknesses (Heb. 4:15). In Him is strength!

Ruth Gleaning in the Fields
to Care for Naomi and Herself

"So Ruth the Moabitess said to Naomi, 'Please let me go to the field, and glean heads of grain after him in whose sight I may find favor.' And she said to her, 'Go, my daughter'" (Ruth 2:2). Ruth was not sure in which field she would be received. She probably felt that in many places she would be chased away, for she was a Moabitess. The law, however, gave her some protection. It required that harvesters not take all the grain but leave gleanings in the field for the poor, whether Israelites or foreigners (Lev. 23:22). When she added, "after him in whose sight I may find favor," she was saying, in effect, that she was living the life of a pilgrim.

At times the Lord brings us into situations that are hard to understand, but these are the times we should seek the Lord for His mercy. When we are no longer assured of our source of supply, we really begin to seek the Lord. For example, it is not until college students graduate that they confront the real thing. Until then, they are sheltered by their parents' money or by financial aid. They think that after graduating, they will find a way. They will, but they should never believe that any situation is rock-solid. Even the companies that appear most stable can fold in a matter of months. There are times when the Lord will make it evident that we must trust in Him and not in anything else.

Here in Ruth 2 is a sweet exchange between a mother-in-law and her daughter-in-law. Ruth did not say, "Old woman, you have nothing to eat. I guess I need to find some food for you, so you don't die of hunger." And Naomi did not say, "Well, get started! I am about to starve to death." Their words were sweet and caring, although both were surely short of food, for that was why they returned to Bethlehem.

Happening upon the Field of Boaz

Ruth "happened to come to the part of the field belonging to Boaz" (Ruth 2:3). I like the words "happened to." It can refer both to things that go in our favor and those that seem to go against us. We Christians should never complain, for everything in our lives "happens to" work together for good (Rom. 8:28). In Ruth's case, she happened to find the field in which she needed to be.

Finding this field is one of the critical matters in our Christian life. Whether our Christian life is prevailing or not is largely determined by what field we have found. What is our field? It is the local church life. We should realize that this field is important, for it is mentioned by the three main people in chapter 2: by Ruth when she asks for Naomi's permission to glean in the field (v. 2), by Boaz when he tells Ruth not to go to another field (v. 8), and by Naomi when she reaffirms that Ruth should not glean in another field (v. 22). The first mentioning of this field is our recognition of the Lord's arrangement that brought us to the field. The second mentioning is the Lord's confirmation that this is the proper field for us. The last mentioning is from those shepherding us; they reaffirm that this is the field where the Lord wants us to be. This field is the church life.

A Field of Barley—Resurrection

The field Ruth gleaned from was a field of barley. In the Bible, barley typifies resurrection. This field represents the church life, which is filled with resurrection. In the church life, we live a life in resurrection. This is amazing. The church life can be the most difficult and even the most impossible life to live on this earth. It is not a smooth way. It is like an intimate family, yet without the bond of flesh and blood. There are endless difficulties. Over and over, it seems we should give up, but for some reason, we are able to forgive and love one another. Everyone interferes in everyone else's business, yet somehow we are able to go on together. Can you honestly say you have had many good days in your church life? Humanly speaking, I would almost advise people to flee from the church life, for it is a most difficult life. Why do we not leave? Because here we have Boaz. "In Him is strength." And here we experience resurrection, for the church is the field where barley grows.

Those in the church life gain the companionship of other believers. As they care for one another, many misunderstandings occur. In an extreme case, suppose someone notices that another's wife seems to have been crying. He asks her if something is wrong, and she does not reply. Fearing the worst, he jumps to the conclusion that her husband has been mistreating her. He begins to ask others if this is the case, and as a result, rumors begin to spread that her husband has been beating her. No one knows that, in fact, she only had sand in her eye. When the husband meets others in the church life, he is greeted with glares. Eventually someone who cares for him says, "You shouldn't hit your wife." When the husband denies it, others do not believe him. How can he endure this kind of misunderstanding? He must find Christ as his resurrection in the church life. It is in these very situations that we discover what resurrection is.

Resurrection is the mark of the church life. What is resurrection? First, resurrection is the defeat of all that belongs to death. Second, resurrection rises above every environment. Third, resurrection is a divine and mystical realm. When we are in resurrection, we experience all three of these. In spite of all the gossip, religious zeal, and intolerance of others, we find that we simply cannot give up. We are upheld and brought into another realm. Once we are brought into resurrection, we are above all that frustrates. Resurrection brings us through incident after incident, case after case, until we are in the heavenlies above every storm. Resurrection is a power that lifts us up into the heavenly realm. This realm is Christ Himself.

The barley field is the church, which is full of resurrection. This resurrection is just Christ, the Head of the church (John 11:25; Col. 1:18). No other person can or should replace Him. The whole sphere, atmosphere, and scope of the church must be nothing and no one but Christ (Col. 3:11). We should all love this field. On the one hand the local church life is so frustrating, yet on the other hand we have to say, "Praise the Lord! In the church life there is Christ as resurrection." The reality, element, and operation of resurrection saturates the church life. It is here that all the aspects of resurrection can be realized.

Gleaning Bit by Bit

When Ruth came to the field of Boaz, she began to glean, that is, to gather bit by bit. According to this picture, we should glean in our field, the church life. If we cannot take in that much, then we should take in a little. We should take from this field according to our capacity. We should stay among the reapers in this field. Some of them cut the grain, some gather it together, and some coordinate for the care and feeding of the workers. This field is the church life where we all labor together according to our function as members in the body.

5

Christ's Care
in the Church Life

In chapter two of Ruth we are introduced to Boaz, a marvelous person. As we have noted, the name Boaz means "in him is strength." Furthermore, Boaz is a man of great wealth. Both his name and his wealth indicate that Boaz, as a type of Christ, is rich and strong to those who know Him as their Lord. He is the all-sufficient One. His riches are unsearchable, and He is able to meet all our need, as long as we attach ourselves to Him. God becomes the strength to all those who are focused upon Christ.

Does this mean that those who trust in Christ will be kept from difficulty or will suffer less than others? No, it does not mean that. Those who know Christ as their Boaz, however, experience being upheld and carried through every kind of difficult situation. It would seem that those who experience such hardships should surrender and give up, but they cannot, for within them is a hidden strength that carries them onward toward God's goal.

Boaz was also the name of one of the two pillars in the temple built by Solomon (1 Kings 7:21). Those who are carried by Christ in His strength find themselves built into His habitation as He strengthens them with might through His Spirit in their inner man (Eph. 3:16). He builds His church by dispensing Himself as the all-sufficient One into His chosen people.

As Ruth sought to care for both Naomi and herself, she "happened to" glean in the field of Boaz (Ruth 2:3). All believers need to find this field. We should not be wanderers, traveling from place to place. If you want to grow well, you should remain in this field. The Lord in His sovereignty arranged that Ruth would happen upon the field of Boaz. After she arrived, Boaz himself charged her further, saying, "Do not go to glean in another field" (v. 8). Afterwards her spiritual mother, Naomi, also counseled her not to be found in any other field (v. 22).

Laboring and Growing in the Field of the Church Life

When I came to the Lord, I spontaneously began laboring in the field of the church life in Taipei. Then one day I left Taiwan to study at a theological school in the United States. After about one week, I realized that this school was not where I should be, so I left. I knew a few Christians who were laboring together in Cleveland, so I joined them, and together we labored in the field of Boaz. What a wonderful field the church life is! Those who are stronger can harvest the grain, and those who are weaker can glean the portion the harvesters leave for them. Concerning Ruth, Boaz told his harvesters, "Let her glean even among the sheaves, and do not reproach her. Also let grain from the bundles fall purposely for her; leave it that she may glean, and do not rebuke her" (Ruth 2:15–16). When I was young, I did not know how to produce anything, but I knew how to follow the older ones. I enjoyed a lot of "leftovers." Eventually I grew, becoming equipped and matured in my operation, until I became a laborer able to produce something for others to enjoy.

The church life is the place for all of us. There is always blessing to be enjoyed in this field. In today's language, the field of Boaz is the expression of the body of Christ where we live. Praise the Lord! Wherever we live, there is a field in which we can labor. If we are weaker, we can receive something from others in this field. If we are stronger, we can labor here so that others have something to eat. As long as we are born again and have a desire for the Lord Himself, we can be satisfied here, for this field produces barley and wheat (Ruth 2:23).

The Significance of the Barley Harvest

Ruth and Noami returned at the time of the barley harvest (Ruth 1:22). Barley in the Bible signifies resurrection. The church life is a life in resurrection. This means that when there seems to be no way to go on, we are still able to rise up and go on. Praise the Lord that there is a field where we can freely labor, and the first grain we reap in this field is barley.

Only in the Lord's field is there a way for everyone to be blessed and to grow. This is the true expression of the body of Christ. The experience of living closely together brings us into resurrection. If this were some other field, we could simply leave this place when we became offended by someone. Sometimes we may feel that a fellow laborer is just too much, but we realize that there is no other place to go. By remaining in this field, we experience resurrection.

In this field, we often feel our Boaz is too much, His young men are too much, and, in fact, the whole thing is too much. Yet we survive, because this is the field where resurrection is found. Sometimes I see the brothers debating and arguing, yet they continue to love one another and cover one another's weaknesses. What makes the church life so precious? The church life has the Lord, the church life has many servants committed to serving together, and this environment results in the experience of resurrection.

Mutual Care in the Church Life

Ruth was greatly blessed. Naomi's God had become her God (Ruth 1:16), and now something spiritual was being imparted to Ruth through Naomi's example. She came to Bethlehem at the time of the barley harvest and happened to glean in the field of Boaz where there was a bountiful supply. There she found many companions who were watchful over her. They seemed to know all about her and reported to Boaz how diligently she had labored among them.

The many servants of Boaz labored together, each carrying out a useful function in a coordinated way. As members of the body of Christ, we are useful to the Lord, and we are a blessing to the body. We should not only be led; we should also lead. We should not only be ministered to; we should minister as well. We should not wait for someone to give us water; we should learn to quench others' thirst. We should exercise and minister in our field just as the workers of Boaz did. Instead of waiting for someone to minister to us for our enjoyment, we should learn to serve others, ministering to their need according to our capacity.

When we feel that the church life has a shortage, the problem is not with others but with our own lack of labor. We idly wait to be watered, nourished, and refreshed, when we ourselves should be laboring with all those around us in this field. In the field of Boaz, some cut the barley, some bind it into sheaves, some cook and serve the food, and some coordinate and oversee others. Each worker contributes to this beautiful portrayal of the church life. How about you—are you laboring in this field according to your ability and capacity? For whom are you caring?

Ruth was a beginner in the church life, yet from the first day she began to serve as best she could. She did not know how to cut or bundle as well as others, but she could at least glean. She could supply both Naomi and herself. She was not waiting to be fed; she was working to feed. She needed to be cared for, but she also cared for someone else. She was served by someone, and she herself served. This is the church life.

So Ruth had Boaz (Christ) as a close kinsman, and she also found his field (the church life). Within this field she found barley (resurrection) and many co-laborers (the brothers and sisters). No one was idle. No one was shirking. All were functioning together by receiving the supply and by ministering it to others. What a good church life!

God Sovereignly Arranges All Things
for Growth in Life

Naomi's husband had a wealthy relative named Boaz (Ruth 2:1). Ruth happened to glean in this man's field. Through this seemingly chance occurrence, she realized that God was in control. In this universe, there is only one who is in charge, and that is God. For us, there is nothing called lucky or unlucky; it is God's hand that determines all things. God arranges all things so that we might partake of divine blessings.

Many times a seemingly small occurrence can change our lives. When we believe in the Lord, many such things begin to happen to us due to the Lord's governmental activity in our environment. The Lord arranges everything for our profit. We should not say, "What a lousy boss (or teacher or professor) I have!" Every detail in our lives has been tailored by God for us to know the Lord and to gain Him. If we do not know how to appreciate what the Lord has done, we will not be able to enter fully into what the Lord has prepared for our benefit. If we appreciate the Lord's arrangement, many things in our experience will become steps of life. Without this realization, we will merely pass through things without gaining much profit from them.

The Lord's arrangement in our environment should bring us through many steps of life. For instance, when we enter elementary school, that is a step of life. When we graduate from junior high and enter into high school, that is another step of life. When we begin our first job, that is yet another step of life. This same principle applies to our spiritual life. We are passing through stage after stage of spiritual growth. I pray that through these words you will not just receive some teaching or knowledge. I hope you will be able to say, "I have gained something further of the Lord. I have been brought into another realm of experience with Christ."

Once we begin to follow the Lord, the first thing we must acknowledge is the Lord's divine arrangement of all things in our life. We will then say, "Lord, my life is in Your hands. My future is in Your hands. In all things, You are the One who is in control."

Sweet Fellowship in the Church Life

When Boaz arrived at his field, he greeted his workers by saying, "The Lord be with you," and his workers responded by saying, "The Lord bless you" (Ruth 2:4). How sweet this church life is! So many are laboring in this field, yet they do so in such an atmosphere. Their unique focus is the Lord. How good it would be if we would always greet one another in this way! Those who are under the Lord's sovereign hand, those who have experienced His faithful dealing as they trust in Him, can fellowship with one another in this way. This is the mark of the church life. "The Lord be with you....The Lord bless you." We must have the Lord.

Obtaining a Good Report

Boaz inquired of his foreman regarding Ruth. She possibly had introduced herself to this overseer and explained her situation to him. He testified to Boaz on her behalf that she had been laboring continuously among the workers since morning. She was a hard worker. She only rested when necessary. May we all pick up this virtue, giving ourselves to our divine commitment tirelessly until the day we give account to the Lord (Rom. 14:12).

Boaz Assuring and Encouraging Ruth

At this point, Ruth experienced Boaz's own concern and comfort. He said to her, "You will listen, my daughter, will you not? Do not go to glean in another field, nor go from here, but stay close by my young women" (Ruth 2:8). Our field is the church life. We should enjoy the church life where the Lord has sovereignly placed us. Just as Ruth was instructed to stay close by the young women, we also need companions; we should not be solitary Christians. Boaz continued, "Let your eyes be on the field which they reap, and go after them" (v. 9). We should be watchful to see where the reaping is taking place so that we can pick up the food as it becomes available. We should keep our eyes on Christ and on those who are pioneering ahead of us. In this way, we will receive the blessing.

Boaz also told Ruth that he had charged his young men not to bother her, and that she was free to drink the water provided for his laborers (2:9). When you become thirsty in the church life, remember that there are fellow believers who are able to provide water for you. Learn how to partake of the rich provision that the Lord makes available to you in the body.

Upon hearing all of Boaz's kind words, Ruth fell on her face before him and asked, "Why have I found favor in your eyes, that you should take notice of me, since I am a foreigner?" (v. 10). Ruth was not just a foreigner; she was a despised Moabitess. Yet Boaz replied that he had heard about Ruth's care for her mother-in-law and how she left her homeland and journeyed to a strange country. Boaz testified on her behalf; she did not testify of herself. Too often we broadcast every experience we have. We might say, "Lord, don't You know how I have paid this price and followed You? You seem to be unaware." The Lord responds, "Although I appear not to be aware, I am fully aware. I am intimately acquainted with your situation." We should allow the Lord to testify on our behalf.

Boaz also said of Ruth that she should be recompensed by the Lord for her work, for she had come to take refuge under the Lord's wing (v. 12). Ruth had not merely believed in Naomi's God and returned with Naomi, but she had also come under the Lord's protecting wings. She had come to know God personally. Our Lord knows all that we have done, and He also knows how to recompense those who have paid the price to follow Him. From my own experience I know this is true. My children had to go through certain things as I followed the Lord, including a time when they had to go to a school where everything was taught in Chinese. That was difficult for them and for us as parents, for they were raised in the United States and did not speak Chinese. I told the Lord that He had to educate them. Eventually they all received postgraduate degrees from excellent universities. The Lord truly knows how to recompense those who are willing to sacrifice everything to follow Him.

This is the Christian life. Tell the Lord that you love Him and you want to give your whole life to Him. He will recompense you with Himself for eternity.

Boaz's Care Reaching Ruth

Ruth replied to Boaz, "Let me find favor in your sight, my lord; for you have comforted me, and have spoken kindly to your maidservant, though I am not like one of your maidservants" (2:13). Ruth surely wished she were like Boaz's maidservants. When she first arrived with her mother-in-law, she could not have been very restful, for nothing of their future was assured. Perhaps Ruth was anxiously considering what would become of them. She had no husband, and she was a foreigner, which meant that she had no provider and no portion among the people with whom she found herself. She was with an old and seemingly helpless widow for whom she had to provide as well. Now, however, Ruth was comforted by this wealthy stranger who happened to be a close kinsman of her deceased husband and father-in-law.

Boaz invited her to eat with his reapers, and he himself extended some food to her. It would seem that she must have been sitting very near him, but we are told that she sat next to his reapers. How could he, the master, have reached all the way over to her, the one who was sitting far away from him? I think we all have experienced our Lord's long reach in His care for us. We often feel as though we are too far from the Lord to receive anything from Him. He is in the center, and we feel we are in the furthest row back. Yet He says, "Here is something just for you," and He reaches right to where we are. The blessing comes directly to us. We may feel that we do not know where the Lord is, but His hand always has a way to find us.

A Common Portion and a Particular Portion

After Ruth ate and was satisfied, she still had something left over (Ruth 2:14). Whenever we enjoy the Lord, there is always something more. Furthermore, Boaz charged his young men, saying, "Let her glean even among the sheaves, and do not reproach her. Also let grain from the bundles fall purposely for her; leave it that she may glean, and do not rebuke her" (vv. 15–16). This is how satisfying the Lord is to us in the church life. First, we have been placed here through God's sovereignty. Second, we are comforted by the Lord's assurances. Third, we are satisfied by His plentiful supply. It would seem that Ruth was even encouraged to take something from Boaz that she was not entitled to—and probably would not have had the boldness to take—so he had his young men "let grain from the bundles fall purposely for her."

The Hebrew word translated "bundles" in verse 16 is unique in the entire Bible. What is the significance of this? I believe it means that there are two kinds of blessing apportioned to us. One is general and is shared and enjoyed by all who follow the Lord. This is our common blessing. The other, however, is special and unique to each individual believer. This is the special blessing. On the one hand, we all share the same Lord, the same salvation, and the same satisfaction and enjoyment in Christ as the portion of the saints in the light (Col. 1:12). On the other hand, in our development and growth, we experience many things that become uniquely ours. From these "bundles" come many ministries. Every ministry belongs to the one to whom it was given to develop. What fell from those particular bundles was Ruth's alone. That was her specific portion.

An Abundant Blessing
Becoming Another's Nourishment

What came to Ruth that day was far more than she could have imagined or hoped for. With us it is the same. The Lord arranges something for us far beyond anything we could ever anticipate. It is as if He says, "When I want to bless you, I go beyond all established principles. I will freely and abundantly bless you." Eventually from her day's work Ruth was able to beat out an entire ephah of barley (Ruth 2:17). When she returned to Naomi, she had this ephah of barley as well as what she had left over from her meal with Boaz and his workers. Remember, even if we cannot digest all that we receive, it still can become food for others. We may not be able to receive much more than ten minutes of enjoyment when we read the Bible for an hour, but that hour's worth of reading will eventually reach someone who needs it.

Naomi's Response to Boaz's Kindness

Naomi asked Ruth from whom had she received such kindness and bounty. Ruth replied that the man's name was Boaz. Once Naomi heard this, she seemed to be clear how things would unfold from that point onward. She said, "Blessed be he of the Lord, who has not forsaken His kindness to the living and the dead" (Ruth 2:20). Naomi was truly spiritual. She realized that Ruth's meeting Boaz was God's provision to redeem for them their inheritance in the land and to raise up children in the name of her son, Ruth's late husband (4:10).

Resurrection, Then Death

In Ruth 2:23 we are told, "So she stayed close by the young women of Boaz, to glean until the end of barley harvest and wheat harvest; and she dwelt with her mother-in-law." In this short portion much is conveyed. The barley harvest commenced after the Passover and the feast of unleavened bread. During this time, the firstfruit of barley was offered to the Lord as a wave offering. The wheat harvest was associated with the feast of Pentecost, which took place fifty days after the feast of the firstfruits (Lev. 23:4–21). Barley is associated with resurrection, while wheat is symbolic of the Lord's death on the cross. In this portion, resurrection is portrayed first, and afterwards death.

We must experience the Lord's resurrection before we are able to enter into the experience of the Lord's death. This matches the order in Philippians, where Paul tells us he sought to "know Him and the power of His resurrection, and the fellowship of His sufferings, being conformed to His death" (3:10). The more we experience the Lord's resurrection, the more we are strengthened to take the pathway of the cross. The more we are enlivened by the Spirit, the more we are enabled to experience the Spirit's work of termination.

During Pentecost, the firstfruit of wheat was offered to the Lord. This indicates that you have reached another stage in your experience of Christ. You are not merely regenerated; you also experience the Spirit's leading and filling. You belong to the Spirit. Not only do you reap in resurrection (signified by the Feast of Firstfruits), but you are also filled with the Spirit (signified by the feast of Pentecost—Acts 2:1–4). You can then die with Christ. First you experience resurrection, next you are filled in spirit, and then you enter into the experience of Christ's death and die with Christ. First you experience the barley, and then the wheat.

The more we are filled in spirit, the more the Spirit saturates us; the more we are enlivened, the more we have the ability to say, "I die with Christ." Chapter two concludes with Ruth harvesting not barley, but wheat. The wheat harvest concludes with the Feast of Tabernacles, or Booths. In other words, as we advance in this stage, we have a testimony that our life is within the tent. We are not of this world. We belong to Christ alone. No one can say how long the experience of the Lord's death in us is required. One day, however, the Lord will gather everything together. Resurrection has already been accomplished by Christ, but the outworking of His death in us is for our lifelong experience. Some progress quickly, others slowly. There was a specific time in our life when we partook of Christ's resurrection, but as to experiencing His death, we all are still on the way. The Lord just tells us we must grow. Nobody can grow for you. You yourself must enter into this process and complete it. One day the Lord will gather all, and that is the Feast of Ingathering, the Feast of Tabernacles.

6

Finding Christ under God's Arrangement

The first two chapters of Ruth tell us much about our Christian experience. In chapter two, we have three parties: Naomi, Ruth, and Boaz. Naomi was mature and cared about Ruth's welfare. Ruth was able and willing to receive Naomi's direction. Boaz took care of them both out of his rich supply. If we desire to become mature, we must not only have Christ as the source of the rich supply, but also a mature one who knows how to help us and guide us in matters relating to Christ.

Maturing in Christ under the Guidance of a Naomi

In chapter three of Ruth, we see a picture of someone maturing in Christ. Ruth has passed through much already. She has gleaned until the end of the barley harvest and the wheat harvest (Ruth 2:23). Through a period of time, she has partaken of many experiences of barley, symbolizing the Lord's resurrection, and wheat, symbolizing His death. In the church life, we experience the power of the Lord's resurrection and being conformed to His death (Phil. 3:10). After a certain amount of experience, we become a relatively mature member in the church life. Even so, we need the experiences depicted in chapter three.

I have been impressed by a particular hymn. I always thought it was written by someone with a rich experience of Christ, like

Watchman Nee. To my surprise, I discovered it was written by a young sister. When I was visiting England, I purposely visited the place where she once lived so I could learn something about her. I later discovered that she never produced another hymn equal to that one. Why is this? It is because she never had anyone who could guide her, so she never was able to grow as she might have.

I am thankful that Watchman Nee had Margaret E. Barber to guide him and that Witness Lee had Watchman Nee. There should always be someone more experienced than we are who can shepherd and guide us in so many respects.

Young people love independence. They like to plan their own path. But a young person without a Naomi will find it difficult to grow properly.

I am close to seventy years of age. I began following the Lord when I was seventeen. Since that time, my life has revolved around the church. If you were to ask me what rich blessings I have received in my life, I would have to say, besides the Lord, the Word, and the church life, I have been blessed by certain Naomis.

If it were not for the Naomis, our church life would degenerate to a social club. The people we know best are those in the church life. Those to whom we can talk are here. Therefore, it is easy to make the church life merely a social life. Once this happens, it will have a goal other than Christ. When we are in the church life for social reasons more than for Christ, we will miss Christ and end up in something apart from Christ.

A Testimony of Some Naomis

Let me illustrate. When I was a young Christian, an older brother who cared for me invited me to join a training for brothers learning to minister. I was one of the youngest ones present. After each brother shared a gospel message that he had prepared, the others critiqued his sharing. I prepared for my turn, and after I shared, I felt quite happy. The others also felt that I had done a good job. Then this older brother said, "I do not understand. You spent a lot of time telling us a story, but you never told us how it ends. Your disposition seems to be quite loose. From now on, I strongly advise you to live a life disciplining yourself." I cannot tell you how much that word helped me. It changed my entire operation. We all need such a Naomi.

This same brother also helped me later in my serving life. At one point, there was trouble brewing among the churches in Taiwan after a brother had visited there and given a conference. This brother who was caring for me set up a time with me. During that time, he said, "A brother I greatly respect once told me a story about Watchman Nee, saying that he seemingly didn't do something so well. Titus, what would you do if you were in my place? How would you react to this brother and his story?" My blood started to boil. I was tempted to say something, when that brother looked at me sternly and said, "Titus, it is *none of your business*." That word saved me. Many of the leading brothers at that time were siding with one brother against another. Had I not received this word, I might have become entangled and taken sides in the controversy. Instead, I was preserved. That storm lasted at least eight years. Do you know why I am still here? Because I had a Naomi.

After I came to the United States, Witness Lee became my Naomi. One day he found me reading a Chinese Bible and said, "Titus, are you still reading the Bible in Chinese?" In other words, I was in the United States, and I needed to develop my ability to use the English Bible. From that time on, I began to study many different editions of the English Bible. Eventually I learned from him something about the English translations and their comparative usefulness.

Naomi's Concern for Ruth's Profit

In this passage in Ruth 3, Naomi says, "My daughter, shall I not seek security for you, that it may be well with you?" (v. 1). Naomi was concerned about Ruth's state. She cared for her security, well-being, and development.

Some care for others by merely bringing them into programs. They try to get them plugged into something. That is not the way that Naomi took care of Ruth. She sought what was best for her according to her particular need, considering what was profitable to Ruth. We each need someone to love us in this way.

In Ruth 3:2 Naomi told Ruth, "Now Boaz, whose young women you were with, is he not our relative?" In other words, do you not have a living Christ? And do you not have companions in the church life? "In fact, he is winnowing barley tonight at the threshing floor." Winnowing is the process by which the wind is used to separate the shell of threshed grain from its kernel. Barley signifies resurrection, but resurrection cannot be fully realized as long as there are shells. When the shell is winnowed away, then the life, or fruit, of barley is manifested and can be dispensed into people.

Boaz, who represented the Lord, was going to do something at that time, and Naomi, who cared for Ruth, knew what he would do. On the one hand, Ruth had passed through some experiences of gleaning wheat and barley. She had a level of maturity that she had not possessed before. On the other hand, she needed some further perfecting. Boaz was moving, and Ruth was ready. Naomi was the unique one who could put these two together. To have the ability to recognize this opportunity and act on it was not a small thing.

Knowing Both the Lord and Those We Serve

Naomi could have been content to receive the grain that Ruth had been collecting under Boaz's generosity. They might have accumulated quite a portion by that time. They might have been comfortable, even well-off. If Naomi had not cared for Ruth's further perfecting, she might have been happy with what Ruth was producing. Ruth had gleaned through at least two harvests; she had a good job with a steady income. Spiritually, we might say to one we are with, "Praise the Lord! He has blessed you bountifully, and you are experiencing a sweet church life." Perhaps Ruth kept bringing home her ephah of grain daily. There was blessing. In the church life, perhaps this could be interpreted as increase or enrichment. But Naomi was not controlled by this; she was concerned with Ruth's continual progress. In actuality, Ruth was dying. Apparently she was doing well, but if she could not take the next step prepared for her, she would begin to languish. Therefore Naomi was watching desperately for an opportunity for Ruth to take this next step.

As we serve others, we must have these two abilities. On the one hand, we must know the situation of those we serve. What is the next step they need to take? On the other hand, for the sake of their advancement, we must be able to see how the Lord is moving. Then we must act at the proper time. How is the Lord working? He is winnowing His barley; He is releasing the full power of His resurrection. If we know how to spot this operation of the Lord, and if we recognize the readiness of the ones we are caring for to participate in it, then the resurrected Lord can move richly among us in the church life. All the shells will be cast off, and the reality of resurrection will be powerfully manifested. Naomi saw both Ruth's need and Boaz's move, just as we should see the need of those we are caring for and the Lord's current move.

Naomi's Advice

Naomi gave Ruth some specific advice. She seemed to be saying, "Ruth, sit up straight and listen carefully to what I tell you now. You must find security, and for this you must develop. Boaz is moving, and now is the time to take action. Here's what you must do: First of all, wash yourself. Second, anoint yourself and change your clothes. Third, go down to the threshing floor. Fourth, hide yourself until Boaz is finished eating and drinking. Fifth, when he falls asleep, uncover his feet and lie down. In the end, he will tell you what to do."

Being Cleansed

First, Naomi told Ruth to wash herself. This surely implies the cleansing of sin. For this you must either confess (1 John 1:9) or walk in the light as He is in the light (v. 7). Confess your sins as you come to the Lord, and if He gives you no feeling to confess anything in particular, tell Him, "Lord, I am a sinner saved by grace. I come to Your presence to enjoy You and to partake of You." Sometimes, though you may not have spent time alone with the Lord, you still experience cleansing as you fellowship with others. You feel refreshed and ready to pursue the Lord again. Learn to come to the Lord privately to confess your sins, and learn also to come to the light through fellowship with others.

Being Anointed and Clothed

Then Ruth was to anoint herself and change her clothes. What do the anointing and the clothing refer to? In Ezekiel 16:8–9, the Lord tells of how He spread His skirt over Israel and covered her nakedness. The clothes in Ruth and the skirt in Ezekiel refer to the same thing. Then He says, "I swore an oath to you and entered into a covenant with you, and you became Mine....Then I washed you in water; yes, I thoroughly washed off your blood, and I anointed you with oil." Here the Lord says that He covered them, washed them, and anointed them with oil. In the Bible, the anointing abides in us and implies consecration (1 John 2:27; Exo. 30:30). From Ezekiel we see that we need a consecration that is based upon His covering, washing, and anointing. This consecration is not based upon our ability but upon Christ's redemptive work.

According to Ezekiel 16, the covering, the washing, and the anointing are all accomplished by the Lord. How do we come to the Lord? We come based upon His covering for our protection, His washing for our redemption, and His anointing for His constituting work within us. We come to the Lord bringing what

He has worked upon us and within us.

Sometimes we feel prevailing and hopeful. Maybe we have just given a good testimony. We feel so acceptable at that time. Or maybe we feel our years as a Christian have made us more acceptable to the Lord than others who seem further down the ladder. No, we should only bring to the Lord and consecrate to Him what He has done in us. The clothing we wear must be the Lord Himself, who has become our covering and the constitution of our living. Clothing in the Bible often typifies our living and behavior. When we come to the Lord, we must realize that we have nothing to brag about. Instead we must say, "Lord, I have loved You so many years, but all that I can bring is what You have worked into me as my clothing, washing, and anointing. Something of You is now in me, and this is all that I have with which to meet You."

In chapter one, Ruth gave herself according to what she had seen of God. In chapter three, she gives herself according to the God whom she has experienced. Don't you have something of the Lord by this time? Do not bring your natural being, your natural man, your natural talent, or your natural zeal to the Lord in your effort to please Him. You must prepare yourself with what He has constituted of Himself into you.

Going Down to the Threshing Floor

After all this, Ruth had to go down to the threshing floor. From this point, her experience would be in darkness, in the night. We might have expected that, as a Christian following the Lord, we would be in the enjoyment all the time. Actually, from the time we gave ourselves to the Lord in this way, we began to enter into death, suffering, misunderstanding, defamation, and difficulties. This happens because of our desire to follow the Lord and Him alone.

In Ruth 3:13–14, Boaz tells Ruth to sleep there until dawn. How long will this be in our experience? We cannot say for sure, but there is a prolonged period during which the Lord is waiting for us to mature. During this time, others will misunderstand us. We will appear too extreme to them, as Jesus did when His family thought that He was "out of His mind" (Mark 3:21). Someone in our family might say, "It is one thing to go to theological school, or even to serve the Lord full-time, but don't give yourself to the Lord in such an absolute way. Don't be like the Lord, who gave Himself." Enduring this kind of suffering that the Lord Himself endured is a time of night. We are still waiting for that dawn. Even though we suffer misunderstanding, there is a kind of joy now, for we know that from this time on, besides the Lord, there will be no one else. Ruth could no longer consider marrying anyone else. She would not live for anyone else. This became her realization during that night as she lay quietly at his feet.

Noticing Where He Lies Down

Naomi told Ruth not to make herself known to Boaz until he had finished eating and drinking. This is the experience of those who offer back to the Lord in their consecration what He has worked into them. Some believers publicly announce their consecration in a showy manner even before telling the Lord about it. Real consecration is transacted privately before the Lord and then lived out. Many believers never experience this. They spend hours talking on the phone but have very little communication with the Lord. Furthermore, they are pushy and insistent with the Lord. Rather than patiently allowing Him to have His enjoyment first, they complain, whine, and insist that the Lord do something for them immediately. In this deeper consecration, however, it is the Lord who has become the center, not we ourselves.

Then, we take note of where the Lord lies down. This is where we must go to consecrate ourselves to the living person of Christ, not anywhere else. We cannot just lie down in the field and say, "Praise the Lord, I am in the church life!" We have to come to the exact place where the Lord is.

When I was young, I gave myself to the Lord for the church. Today, I am in the church life for the Lord. Eventually we all must be able to say, "Lord, I love You. I am only following You. Where You lie down, I lie down at Your feet. I am not worthy, nor am I qualified. It is all Your mercy."

We have to marvel at Ruth's obedience to Naomi. If I were Ruth, I would have been filled with questioning and apprehension. "Clothes? Which clothes? And what if I go there and I cannot find Boaz? And if I do, what if he sees me and kicks me out? Or if I am able to find him and sleep there, what if he should wake up and get upset with me? I would feel that my life was over, having slept at the feet of a man all night. Naomi, your advice doesn't make sense. Aren't we living comfortably now?" Isn't this what many of us experienced when we consecrated ourselves absolutely to the Lord? Were we not satisfied as functioning members in the church life? So many are doing fine in the church life, but they refuse to follow Christ. The mature ones in the church life must be focused only upon Christ.

Ruth's Response

Ruth possessed something precious, for her reply to Naomi was, "All that you say, I will do." Then she went to the threshing floor and found Boaz there, just as Naomi had said she would.

Boaz Lying Down
at the End of the Heap of Barley

The Bible tells us that Boaz, after eating and drinking, was cheerful (Ruth 3:7). Perhaps he sensed intuitively that something wonderful was about to take place. After finishing his meal, he went to lie down at the end of the heap of barley. Boaz did not lie down at the highest point of his mound of grain. This signifies that the Lord, even though He is in resurrection, is still able to reach us where we are. The mound of barley signifies resurrection. The Lord lies down in an accessible spot very close to us while still in resurrection. He doesn't depart from His resurrection; He remains in resurrection, yet is still in a place where we can find Him. Because of this, we have a way to approach Him, as Ruth was able to approach Boaz.

As Boaz lay asleep at the edge of the heap of grain, Ruth stole in, uncovered his feet, and lay down. Everything took place as Naomi had said it would. Isn't this marvelous? When those who care for us tell us the way to find the Lord, we should feel confident that the Lord will bless us accordingly.

Boaz Startled at Ruth's Presence

At midnight, Boaz was startled at Ruth's presence. We can imagine him stretching out his leg and suddenly discovering someone else lying there. He was startled. I like this. In a positive sense, we have the ability to startle the Lord. Isn't this wonderful? In the Song of Songs 4:9, the king tells the Shulamite, "You have ravished my heart, my sister, my spouse; you have ravished my heart with one look of your eyes, with one link of your necklace." When the Lord sees us, He somewhat loses His composure. We are so attractive to Him!

Sometimes when we pour out our hearts to Him, He is constrained by us. He sees the beauty of our humanity inwrought with divinity, and He is captured. His breath is taken away by what He sees in us. We are lovely to Him. Perhaps when He realizes how much we love Him, He is startled. I like this. The more I can startle Him in this way, the happier I will be. We should not be so common in His eyes; our relationship with Him must become one of allurement.

When Boaz discovered Ruth at his feet, risking everything, including her reputation, he asked her, "Who are you?" I somewhat believe that he knew, but he was in a state of marveling. Ruth replied, "I am Ruth, your maidservant. Take your maidservant under your wing, for you are a close relative" (Ruth 3:9). Ruth seemed to be saying, "I already belong to you. Now marry me. You have taken me in; now complete what you have begun." Boaz was a close relative to the husband Ruth had lost, and it was Boaz's duty to raise up children in the name of her dead husband (Deut. 25:5). Boaz had already spoken of how she had come to Israel to seek protection under the wing of Jehovah (Ruth 2:12). He was confident that Jehovah would recompense her. Now she had taken refuge under Boaz's wing, as if to remind him of his words, in addition to what she plainly meant— "Marry me."

We need such a desirous heart toward the Lord. On the one hand, we should lay aside all that we have: our hopes, aspirations, dreams, expectations, and desires. On the other hand, we should place ourselves and our future firmly at the Lord's mercy. We should give ourselves to Him alone, not based upon anything we have, but fully upon the work He has already begun in us. Then we should take the opportunities that the Lord gives us to grow to fullness under the direction of those who have the ability to discern both our condition and how the Lord is moving. In this kind of situation, we should lay hold of the Lord. We should be direct with Him for His testimony's sake. It is no longer for our sakes that we seek Him; it is for what is on His heart. We are asking Him for what He wants, and this startles Him.

A Mutual Blessing

Ruth was saying, "Boaz, you recognized that I had come to take refuge under Jehovah's wing. That wing is your wing. Therefore, take your maidservant under your wing." Boaz responded, "I will do all that you ask. Have no fear. Your gamble was safe with me, for you are right. I am your close relative. You think *you* are blessed, but actually you are becoming a blessing to *me*."

Boaz had already blessed Ruth by supplying her needs. Based upon that, Ruth had matured, but she still needed to take another step. Under Naomi's wise care, she found Boaz and entered into a relationship with him in which he became her center. No longer was she merely dependent upon him for some supply. From now on, she would learn to know him as her center and her everything, moving when he moved, being joined to him to bring forth something for his heart's desire.

7

Preparation
in the Night

In Ruth chapter three, Naomi directed Ruth in a very specific manner, for she realized that the time had come for Ruth to enter into what would bring her rest. Naomi really cared for Ruth. Even though it meant she might lose everything, she cared more for Ruth's well-being than for her own. She fought for Ruth and acted with Ruth's welfare in view. Her intention was to find what would bring rest to Ruth (3:1, KJV). That rest for Ruth was a person—Boaz. Many times we may hold on to certain people because we feel they are profitable to us and to the church. If we care for what they can do for us more than for their spiritual growth, we frustrate the church from realizing the greater blessing that comes with their growth. We should be for others' profit and consider what is best for them rather than how they might be of help to us.

Naomi realized that the next stage of growth for Ruth was finding rest with Boaz. We should care for those with us in the same way. Has the person of Christ become their rest to the degree that He should?

Naomi's Instructions to Ruth

Naomi directed Ruth according to her knowledge of what Boaz was doing. She knew that he was winnowing his barley at his threshing floor during the night. This is very meaningful, for our thought is often that the Lord's activity is in the glorious light of day. When the Lord truly moves, however, it is often during the night. If you desire to find Him, you will be brought into trials, sufferings, and difficulties. In this atmosphere, all that prevents the full expression of resurrection can be removed. Winnowing removes the shells that cover the seed. By passing through the winnowing process of the night, the resurrection life represented by the barley can come forth more richly and become a blessing to anyone who touches it. By passing through the night experiences, resurrection life becomes powerfully manifested.

Naomi told Ruth to wash, anoint herself, and change her clothes before going to Boaz. Ruth's purpose in going to Boaz was to offer herself to him. According to Ezekiel 16:8–9, the washing, anointing, and clothing are provided by the Lord. This reveals that our offering ourselves to Christ must be based upon what Christ has wrought into us. Our natural strength, ability, and zeal are not acceptable. What we offer to Christ must be what Christ Himself has wrought into us. After we are cleansed by Him, we must offer what He has worked into us through our years with Him. The constitution of the divine attributes within us becomes the capital for us to come into the Lord's presence in this way.

We realize that our fallen nature will always be with us until the day we fully enter into resurrection with the Lord. Fifty years ago, I thought that as I grew older I would become very holy and free of defilement. Now, fifty years later, I discover that there is more defilement instead of less, yet I also discover that I have much more of the Lord's anointing. I have experienced so much cleansing and anointing, and the Lord has given me a colorful garment in the process. This is what we should bring with us when we come into the Lord's presence.

Watching Boaz and Waiting for an Opportunity

We know that the events of chapter three do not immediately follow those of chapter two, for there has been at least one wheat harvest after the initial barley harvest (Ruth 2:23). After partaking of these harvests (representing the experience of the Lord's resurrection and death), and after being washed, anointed, and clothed in this way, in the dark night we must come to our Boaz on the threshing floor in a hidden way. We do not declare our experience or anything that we have. Instead, we hide ourselves. In the previous chapter, Ruth stood forth. In this experience, however, she must learn to stay hidden. When we offer ourselves to the Lord in this way, we are not seeking enjoyment in the church life; we are seeking Christ Himself.

In this experience, we wait for Christ's time. We do not ask Him to fit ours; we simply watch Him. After He is finished eating and drinking, He will do as He wishes. Now what we do is according to His schedule, not ours. We watch now to see what pleases Him. We watch His move. We notice where He lies down. We cannot afford to lose sight of Him. When Ruth saw where Boaz lay down, she stole in, uncovered his feet, and placed herself at his feet. This was as far as Naomi's instructions could take her. She realized that at that point, it was in Boaz's hands. At a certain point, after we have prepared and done what we should do, the Lord must take over. We are responsible to offer ourselves and focus upon Him. He is responsible to accomplish what He desires upon us.

I am concerned for the young people. They have been so strongly influenced to seek independence. Ruth said to Naomi, "All that you say to me I will do" (Ruth 3:5), but how many among us today are so responsive to the lead of those who are older? Often they are seen as out-of-date. In today's society, young people often do not even listen to their parents. Ruth's example portrays a great secret in the spiritual life. We must recognize the order in the body. Our spiritual growth will be determined by our attitude toward those whom the Lord has placed spiritually ahead of us.

Startling Boaz

As Ruth waited quietly, Boaz finished eating and drinking.

When his heart was merry, he went to lie down at the end of the heap of barley. She then came in secretly and uncovered his feet and lay down. At midnight, Boaz awoke and was startled to find Ruth there. When we love the Lord in this way and pursue Him, we sometimes startle Him. He is amazed at us. I was once a naughty boy of seventeen who played hooky for a whole semester. Now, after years of the Lord's beautifying work, I am able to kneel down and tell the Lord Jesus, "I love You." Oh, I am satisfied, and I know the Lord is startled by my presence.

Ruth's Bold Request

Boaz said to Ruth, "Who are you?" She replied that she was his maidservant and quickly added, "Take your maidservant under your wing, for you are a close relative" (Ruth 3:9). In other words, "According to the Lord's commandment, you should marry me, for you are a close relative of my husband." The wing of Boaz was, to Ruth, the wing of Jehovah that Boaz spoke of in 2:12. Ruth seemed to be saying, "Spread your wing over your maidservant. You said that I came to seek refuge under Jehovah's wing. Now I am taking refuge under *your* wing as the wing that Jehovah has provided." Today the Lord is spreading His wing over us. He has promised to be our Savior. Based on this we now come to Him and say, "I give my whole being to You so that I may receive Your full salvation. You must become much more than just my Savior. O Lord, I want to take all that You have done, all that You are, and all that You have, and become totally saturated with You. Do You think I am merely coming to You for a refuge? No! I am coming here to possess You."

Not Going After the Young Men

Then Boaz said to Ruth, "Blessed are you of the Lord, my daughter! For you have shown more kindness at the end than at the beginning, in that you did not go after young men, whether poor or rich" (Ruth 3:10). Ruth had been so kind to her mother-in-law by giving up her parents' home and country and accompanying Naomi to a foreign land. Now, however, Ruth wanted to give herself to Boaz rather than to any younger man whom she might marry. The Lord, our Boaz, is all-valuable, all-sufficient, and almighty. He is the Lord of lords and the King of kings. He is the possessor of everything. He is the most desirable One, but often we don't see Him this way, so we are attracted by the young men.

What are the young men? They are the things other than Christ which we pursue and give our lives to. For example, we might let our desire for a position in a company replace Christ. The Lord realizes that from our point of view, that is a premier company. There is a big world out there, with so many appealing things to which we can give ourselves. If we choose Him over these, He appreciates that. Our kindness is manifested in that the world is so attractive, and yet we give up the world to choose Christ. We all must honestly admit, however, that we are glad we have not chosen any of the young men and have rather selected the One who is truly worthy of our life.

The Night Experience

In verse 11, Boaz continues, "And now, my daughter, do not fear." In saying this, Boaz indicated he would marry Ruth, as she desired. In order to do that, however, he had to take care of something first. Ruth was a valued and virtuous woman, and there was a kinsman closer than Boaz who had the first choice in this matter. This must have sounded worrisome to Ruth, so Boaz told her, "Stay this night" (Ruth 3:13). This was a further experience of the night, for it was preparing the way for Ruth's release from this other kinsman to whom she was technically attached. Boaz had to see this kinsman, but it had to be in the morning. Also, if this kinsman exercised his right as her nearest kinsman, Ruth would have to marry him instead of Boaz. For Ruth to marry Boaz, this kinsman must first release his claim on her.

How long is this night experience for us? Six years? Twenty? In our experience there is a long process of growth while we lie submissively at Christ's feet and enjoy His warm protection. Yet during this process we still do not know the release Christ can render or the full experience of oneness with Him.

The Lord's work upon us seems to come most often while we are in the night. Every time we consecrate ourselves, our consecration brings us into the experience of night rather than day. When we declare, "Lord, I give myself to You," He asks, "Are you ready?" If we reply, "Lord, I am," then be prepared. Something that seems disheartening is about to happen. However, at the same time, we sense that the Lord is with us, for we remain at His feet. We sense that He is covering us, but it is still night in our experience.

Ruth lay at his feet until morning. This will be our experience until the Lord returns. We may feel the night is too long. We may complain that we cannot take it any more. When this happens, and we are about to leap up, the Lord will suddenly give us some wonderful daylight. After this experience, the Lord will ask us, "Are you ready to continue?" When we answer, "Yes," the Lord will keep us in the night for a longer time until, once more, we cannot tolerate it. Again, the Lord will encourage us. At first, we can only take a limited period of night experience. Later, the Lord may keep us in the night for a few months. Eventually, He will be able to work with us in this way for a few years. In such a state, we will cry out, "Lord Jesus, Morning Star, come!" (Rev. 22:16–17). The Christian life is a romantic life. We have captured the Lord's heart, but a long way still lies ahead of us. It will not always be a bright, encouraging, smooth, and high road. Yet during this time of night, we experience His protection, for we are covered by His wing.

While it was still dark, when they could just dimly see each other, they arose. Boaz said, "Do not let it be known that the woman came to the threshing floor" (Ruth 3:14). This word was a protection to Ruth. Otherwise, people might spread rumors damaging Ruth's reputation of being a virtuous woman. Boaz cared for Ruth.

Then Boaz said, "Bring the shawl that is on you and hold it" (v. 15), and he measured out to Ruth six ephahs of barley. Ruth's shawl only had a certain capacity. Boaz measured out just that much. Likewise, we can only enjoy a certain amount at one time. Our capacity as human beings is limited.

A Testimony

I would like to tell you a story related to this experience of night and day. Soon after I was saved, I got into a college, but my application landed me in the Boy Scout leader training program. After fellowship with the church elders, I was clear not to attend that school, but instead I applied for an opening as an English interpreter for the military. In the meantime, since I was not attending a university, I had to report for basic training in the military. That was tough. Ten days before basic training was over, I received a letter of acceptance for the interpreter's training program. I was to report for another basic training with them beginning the day after my first basic training concluded. As I sat in the railway car on the way to the interpreter's training camp, I was singing, "The way of the cross means sacrifice." I sang that song all the way from Taipei as the train moved slowly south. Finally, as we were picking up new passengers on the platform, a train stopped from the other direction. As I was there with the Lord, I heard someone call my name. I looked out the window, and there was my company from the previous training, all discharged and in civilian clothes. They were waving at me and calling, "Hey Titus! Here you go again!" I told the Lord, "That's it, Lord. You can hit me and beat me, but You don't have to use sarcasm and make me a laughingstock." I shut my Bible (I dared not tear it up) and my hymnal. After I arrived at my new camp I stored them at the bottom of my footlocker. At every meal I was used to praying, but as I bowed my head for the first time at this place, I suddenly remembered what had happened. So I hardened myself and refused to pray. For about two weeks I did not pray or read the Bible. After such a period of time, however, I just couldn't take it any longer. I missed the Lord too much. I realized that I had better find a place to repent, so I ran all the way to a field and knelt down for about an hour, praying and weeping. I told Him, "Lord, I lied. I told You that I loved You and that I would give my whole being to You. Look at how I gave You up after one little difficulty. Lord, forgive me." I spent a long time confessing before the Lord. That was the first time I realized that every vow we make must be kept by the Lord Himself.

Afterwards I went to the mess hall for supper. The company commander entered with some papers in his hands, looking very sober. At that moment the Lord told me, "Now you can go home." The commander announced, "I have just been instructed by the Department of Defense to release immediately all those who have already passed through basic training for the army. You are to leave at once." The first thing that I realized was how good the Lord was to me. Had I not repented before receiving this news, I would have been too ashamed to stand before the Lord. Even my repentance was something of His mercy.

But there is more to the story. After being discharged, I returned to Taipei. My military-interpreter classes would not start for another three months, so I asked an elder of the church if I could take part in the training that Brother Witness Lee was giving at that time. The elder said he would have to check with Brother Lee, and later he told me Brother Lee wanted to meet me. I was very nervous. When I arrived, Brother Lee simply said, "Oh, you are Titus Chu. Do you have time?" I said yes. Then he just stood before me for a little while, considering before the Lord. Finally he said, "Good. You can come." I was so thankful. The night was over, and my time of blossoming had come! For five months I had been away from the church life. During all that time I had one day off. I had earned the time off by being top in my company, and I had used it to attend a church meeting. I cannot tell you how rich that training was to me. But, believe it or not, about halfway through I became full. I had arrived at my personal "six-bushel" capacity. I had received all that I could receive. I had to pray for the Lord to enlarge me, because so much had happened to me in order to be in that training.

While I was in basic training, a Christian worker had visited Taiwan from England and held some conferences. I received letters describing how glorious those meetings were. That was a torture to me. I felt like a castaway. I prayed, "Lord, why am I not qualified to partake of all these riches?" But if you were to ask me today if I would rather have been in the conference with that brother or in the training with Brother Lee, I would readily respond that I am grateful that I was in the training with Brother Lee. That conference with the other brother brought in much trouble to the churches in Taiwan. I thought I was being deprived, but actually I was being saved. The Lord kept me from that turmoil by means of those months of basic training. How we must love the Lord! I was there for those months, waiting for the dawn. Then came Brother Lee's three-month training. Eventually through all these things my capacity was enlarged.

Some brothers can only handle one meeting. Afterwards they feel so full that they must go to Starbucks for a break. The Lord must use many situations to enlarge us until our capacity to contain the Lord's blessing grows. Then we will become a rich source of supply in the church life. As we mature, our ability to enjoy and receive what the Lord is pouring out becomes greater.

A Shepherd's Reward

While Boaz went into the city to fulfill his word, Ruth returned to her mother-in-law with the six ephahs of barley and told her all that Boaz had done for her. Everything that belonged to Boaz would become Ruth's once they were married, so these six ephahs of barley were really for Naomi, who had cared for Ruth. Naomi had struggled for Ruth's development and had coached her in how to approach Boaz. Naomi's reward for shepherding Ruth was not merely six ephahs of barley. The knowledge that Boaz would marry Ruth as she desired was a far greater reward.

One day in the mid-1960s, I was driving with Brother Lee. Suddenly he turned to me and spoke concerning a particular brother: "Brother Titus, I see a certain amount of maturity with this one." I can never forget how he smiled as he spoke this. He was telling me that this brother, whom the Lord had gained in America through his shepherding, had grown. Many times we do not realize how much the serving ones suffer on our behalf, or the amount of concern they have for us. When we experience a little progress in Christ, how happy they are before the Lord!

As a serving one, I am so comforted when I see those who give themselves to pursue Christ and be found in Him alone. So many are still free to pursue "young men" instead of "Boaz." When we desire to marry Christ alone, those who serve us are comforted. The church life changes as well, because in this transaction, we gain six ephahs of barley with which to feed others. If we take in as much of the riches of Christ as we can (signified by the six ephahs), how encouraged are those who serve us!

In this atmosphere and situation, Naomi said to Ruth, "Sit still, my daughter, until you know how the matter will turn out; for the man will not rest until he has concluded the matter this day" (Ruth 3:18). It was now up to Boaz to take care of matters. There was a closer kinsman who had more right than he, so Boaz had to take care of that. Brothers and sisters, do not fear! Be at peace, for our Boaz will not rest until He has fully done all that He said He would do.

Brought into
Union with Christ

As Ruth chapter three ended, Naomi said that Boaz would not rest until he had finished what he must do that day. Chapter four thus begins with Boaz's dealings with the kinsman who had the first claim upon Ruth and her inheritance. According to Deuteronomy 25:5, the nearest kinsman was responsible for marrying the dead man's wife to raise up children in the name of the deceased. Otherwise the dead man's inheritance in the land of Israel might be lost from his tribe (Num. 36:7–8). This is the purpose of this transaction.

The question now is this: Who does this nearest kinsman represent? It may be argued that Ruth is primarily meant to be a beautiful story, and that doctrines are not a feature of this book. According to this view, when Boaz said, "There is a kinsman closer than I am," it just introduces more tension and romance into the story. However, Boaz clearly represents Christ, and Ruth represents us. Therefore, it must be significant that, though Ruth's desire is toward Boaz and she has given herself to him, there is a kinsman more closely related to her than Boaz.

The Natural Man and Its Pursuit

This nearest relative has the right to declare possession over Ruth. If this is so, how can she offer herself to Boaz at all? In our experience, this closer kinsman is our natural man. If our natural man is our closest kinsman and has the first right of ownership over us, how can we ever be released so that we might be joined to Christ? This kinsman has to be dealt with before we can fully enter into the union we desire with the Lord.

We know our natural man by its desires. What your natural man and my natural man are pursuing may be very different things. We will each pursue what we see as being in our own best interest. If we are bright, our natural man will point us to certain things. If we are ambitious, it will cause us to pursue other things. If we are lazy, it will find us another avenue. The many different fields in the world have developed in response to all the different kinds of people with their abilities and interests. In this way, the world corresponds to the natural man.

Christ as the close relative is in our spirit, which surely desires God Himself. Our natural man, however, as our closest kinsman, is in our soul. In our soul is something called the soul-life, which wants both God and the world. The world exists to match all the desires of the three sections of the natural man: our mind, our emotion, and our will. It is our mind and our emotion that determine which of these two kinsmen will be joined to us.

The Three Sections of the World and Our Natural Man

The world is also of three sections: the sinful section, the material or physical section, and the religious section. The sinful world appeals to our fallen flesh, while the material world appeals to our natural man when we are not focused on Christ alone. Many, for instance, pursue a certain job with a certain company in order to have a certain type of comfortable life.

The "sinful world," as pictured in Ruth, was dealt with in chapter one when Ruth told Naomi, "Wherever you go, I will go...and your God [shall be] my God." (1:16). The "material world" was dealt with in chapter three, when Ruth wholly offered herself to Boaz at the threshing floor.

Because we have been redeemed by Christ, in principle our natural man will no longer choose the sinful aspects of the world.

Nor, in principle, will our natural man desire the material aspect of the world if we have consecrated ourselves to the Lord. What aspect of the world remains for us? This may come as a surprise: It is the "religious world" that has the ability to prevent us from enjoying total union with Christ.

The sinful world is a very close friend of the material world, but the religious world seems separate from the sinful and material worlds, at least in appearance. Initially, believers struggle with the sinful world, and they are repeatedly defeated until they give up. When they give up, however, they seem to find the secret, and thus they are delivered from that aspect of the world. As long as we have the fallen flesh, the allure of the sinful world will remain. However, it will not be the primary thing to which our natural man is attracted. The next level of the world, and one we will find more acceptable, is the material world. Even though we are the Lord's followers, it will still seem reasonable to pursue things in the material world, such as a career or a better lifestyle for our family, more than Christ. A Chinese proverb says that the older you become, the more you will care about money and the less you will care about other things. What tempts me in my old age is the desire for peace and quiet. It would be so pleasant to be delivered from all the turmoils and bothersome things that surround me. But such desires do not own us. We are for Christ.

What is the struggle that will always confront those who have given themselves to Christ? It is the inclination our natural man has toward the things of the religious world. We know that the sinful world and material world are not of Christ. What draws our natural man now is that world where Christ is talked about and yet is absent. The world of religion can fill us with something related to Christ after the living Christ has left. In this way our natural man, with its inclination toward religion, is our closest kinsman.

Simply put, we are controlled by our natural man, and our natural man is controlled by religion. When we believers are living by our natural man, we are controlled by religion more than Christ.

Religion makes people lose some of their ability to reason, for it is governed by zeal, not intellect. It seems that religion should bring people to Christ. However, when people focus on religion, Christ disappears along with reason. In this way our natural man, controlled by religion, becomes our closest relative, even when we desire that our closest relative should be Christ.

The Natural Man's Inclination toward Religion

In religion, people preach about Christ and talk about Him, but Christ Himself is not there. What is it about religion that inclines our natural man so strongly toward it? What makes it so captivating?

The Law

First, religion seems to give the natural man an easy way to please God apart from Christ. We may call this the law. Within every Jesus-lover's natural man, there is a strong inclination toward the law. The natural man says, "I love the Lord. I know what I shall do. I shall memorize 1,000 verses every year." Is there anything wrong with this? Only if we put ourselves under bondage, taking it as a law. Yet even so, our attempt to keep this law will expose our actual situation. When the Israelites at Mount Sinai told Moses, "All that the Lord has spoken we will do" (Exo. 19:8), they ended up dancing around the golden calf before Moses ever came back down from the mountain (32:1–6). This exposing feature is one of the positive functions of the law.

What then shall we do if we cannot set legal goals? If we do not serve the Lord practically, we feel we are not doing what we should. What is wrong with our setting a goal to memorize 1,000 verses a year? Nothing. On the one hand, we will touch Christ in the Word, and on the other hand, if we fail to reach our goal, we will be exposed and brought to Christ to confess our need for Him. If we are able to memorize only five verses this month out of the eighty-four scheduled, we should not fall under the law's condemnation. The natural man seeks justification before God by striving to fulfill the law. The law, however, brings us to Christ through our failure. In this way it is a tutor to bring us to Christ (Gal. 3:24).

Many continue to be held in bondage under the law even though they have Christ. The only way to come out from under the law is to be crucified with Christ. This is seen in Romans 6–7. The law cannot rule over a dead person. Praise the Lord for this!

Ideology

Second, religion provides the natural man with ideology. Christ has given us Himself and so many riches of the truth concerning Himself, yet it is easy for Christians to form all this into an ideology. Once something we have received becomes an ideology, we have departed from Christ.

The Plymouth Brethren are a good illustration of this. In the 1800s, they received so many riches from the Lord. So much light came forth from the Word, and so many rich hymns were written by them. But when what the Lord gave them became an ideology, they lost the living Lord. In Plymouth, England, today, a gathering that once brought the blessing of Christ to thousands has become a meeting of a faithful few who hold onto something with their natural man. That which they are faithfully holding is not Christ but rather a collection of teachings that has become their ideology. We have to be careful of this tendency, for ideology develops so easily. It is much easier to hold onto an ideology than to hold onto Christ. Once ideology is in control, Christ is not.

Some hold onto ideology to the point that they ignore or deny the reality of the body of Christ. For instance, some Christians say they are Lutherans due to their ideology. In fact, they are believers, but they have exchanged the reality of the body of Christ for an ideology. Ideology needs followers; it needs allegiance if it is to be maintained. Among those controlled by ideology, there is no true love which seeks what is best for the entire body of Christ. If we are able to avoid the trap of ideology, we will be so precious in the sight of God. Only this will express the body of Christ.

Self-Confidence and Self-Development

Third, the religious world matches our natural man's desire for self-confidence and self-development. Religion is very good at encouraging us to develop ourselves, and our natural man yearns for such development.

Peter illustrates this. He confidently declared that he had left all to follow the Lord and deserved something in return (Matt. 19:27). Peter's boat and house were no doubt of very little value, even when compared to other boats and houses, yet it seems that he felt no shame in asking what he would get in return for his meager sacrifice. This has always puzzled me. Why are we Christians so confident like this? And why does the Lord receive such declarations from us? We tell Him how much we love Him and that we will give up everything for Him. He never says, "You are lying." We shed tears and confess our love to Him and then immediately leave His presence to do something separate from Him, yet He continues to love us, whether or not we know how to love Him properly in return.

In spite of our behavior, for some reason we are very sure of ourselves. This self-confidence replaces Christ. We trust in our own ability to follow Christ, thinking that we know how to satisfy Him and how to serve Him. We don't. Instead, there is a closer kinsman than Christ, someone closer to whom we yield. That is our natural man, who is attempting to please God apart from Christ. By default, our natural man is our closest kinsman.

Our natural man, which is our closest kinsman, is inclined toward these three aspects of the religious world, each of which replaces Christ. First, our natural man desires to please God by fulfilling the law. Second, he desires to hold onto and defend an ideology. We should only defend the common faith adhered to by all genuine believers, as revealed in the Bible. Third, we are confident that we can do something for Christ. Because our natural man is so close to us, if we are ever to belong to Christ alone, we need Him as our Boaz to take action on our behalf.

Boaz Confronting the Closer Kinsman

In the first verse of Ruth 4, Boaz goes to the gate of the city, and the closest kinsman appears. Boaz has him sit down and then has the elders of the city sit down. I like this picture. The Lord is in charge, and all must obey Him. Even a natural man full of ideology cannot argue in the Lord's presence. Boaz then rehearses how Naomi has returned from the country of Moab without male heirs and is in danger of losing her portion of the land. Boaz presses the kinsman and says, "If you are going to redeem this land, redeem it, for you are the closer kinsman." When we read this, we may get a little nervous, for what would happen to Ruth if this closer kinsman agrees to this? And that is what happens, for this kinsman seems happy to add this property to his own. Boaz reminds him that if he does this, however, he must also marry Ruth and through her raise up a son in her dead husband's name so that his name and inheritance may not come to an end. Hearing this, the closer kinsman balks and is unwilling to fulfill his duty. At this point he surrenders the right to Boaz.

In our experience, when the Lord comes in and confronts our natural man, we listen, but still with our laws, ideology, and self-confidence firmly in place. The Lord says, "You must do this for yourself if you wish to fulfill what is right before God," and initially we are inclined to think we can do it. We see the profit in view. But we do not realize that law, ideology, and self-confidence do not really have our best interest at heart. Rather, we are just a means for the religious world to reach its own ends. Those under law cannot be perfected by the law (Heb. 7:18–19). And those controlled by ideology cleave to something other than Christ. So all that religion represents rears up joyfully within us to lay hold of what seems profitable through the name of Christ. Then the Lord says, "Wait! You must also marry Ruth and raise up an heir for her dead husband for the sake of his place in this land."

Up until this time, the closest relative must have felt very fortunate that Boaz was bringing all this up. It seemed very much to his benefit. But when Boaz brings up the idea of marrying Ruth, this closer relative declines. If the closest kinsman were to have a son by Ruth, it would be required that such a son would belong to Mahlon, the son of Elimelech, and not to himself. That child would be raised up in Elimelech and Mahlon's name and would return to the recovered portion of the land that had belonged to Elimelech. The closest kinsman felt that such a thing would ruin his own inheritance (Ruth 4:6). In other words, he only cared for what he could gain from his association with Ruth. He did not care for her, even though he was closely related to her.

A Heart for One Another's Profit

The religious world uses us; it does not care about us. The Lord, on the other hand, cares for us and fights for what would be a blessing to us. He is struggling for us to mature. He is not taking advantage of us. We are to be His wife (Eph. 5:31–32), and obtaining Him becomes our highest blessing. Religion only seeks to thwart this so that it may maintain and expand its existence with its laws, ideologies, and exaltation of the self.

So the closer kinsman surrendered his right by drawing off his sandal and handing it to Boaz. This was the custom at that time. It was a confirmation, the equivalent of signing a contract today. Boaz then said, "You are witnesses this day that I have bought all that was Elimelech's, and all that was Chilion's and Mahlon's, from the hand of Naomi. Moreover, Ruth the Moabitess, the widow of Mahlon, I have acquired as my wife, to perpetuate the name of the dead through his inheritance, that the name of the dead may not be cut off from among his brethren and from his position at the gate" (Ruth 4:9–10). Boaz was doing this not for his own sake but for Naomi and Ruth, and to perpetuate the name of Elimelech and Mahlon.

When the Lord took us upon Himself, it appears He didn't get anything but a lot of hard work. But at least He got us. The Lord's way is always to pour Himself out and to suffer on our behalf, that we may obtain the ultimate blessing (Eph. 5:25).

To all this the elders and those present said, "We are witnesses." Perhaps they did not understand why Boaz would do such a thing. Ruth was young and possibly beautiful, but Boaz was entering into something that would not bring him any profit in the long run, for any child born of their union would be credited to Mahlon. Boaz would have to work for someone else's profit and raise up a seed for him. How upright, kind, and proper Boaz was! I hope we all would have such a heart to fight for one another's good rather than simply for our own.

At times I have heard some speak critically of those who have left the fellowship. This attitude does not represent God's heart, for He hates to see anyone lose his portion of the enjoyment of Christ. We should not speak of them in this way. Are we somehow heroes since we are thus far able to enjoy the church life? We know it is the Lord's mercy. We stand for the oneness of the body of Christ and are not a sect, yet at times we make ourselves very narrow.

The Blessing upon Ruth and Boaz

Eventually all the people blessed Boaz with an interesting blessing. They said, "The Lord make the woman who is coming to your house like Rachel and Leah, the two who built the house of Israel" (Ruth 4:11). At this I would be insulted, for although Rachel means "sheep," Leah means "weary" or "tired" (Hitchcock). This is like saying, may your bride be like a sheep and like being tired! These, however, are the two who built the house of Israel.

If we desire to build up the Lord's testimony, we must experience what is signified by the names Rachel and Leah. On the one hand, we are Rachel, a lamb consecrated to the Lord for His purpose. Sometimes we strongly declare we are for Him. On the other hand, we are Leah, so weak and weary that it seems we cannot rise up at all. But because of our submission to the Lord, our weakness is that of a consecrated lamb. Because we know Him and because we know ourselves, the Lord has a way to build up His kingdom through us.

The Lord's kingdom is not primarily established through prevailing exercise. No. More often, the Lord's kingdom is built up as we are trusting in Him in the midst of our limitation and weakness. Although we are weak, we are His lambs. Praise the Lord for Rachel and Leah!

Then they continued, "May you prosper in Ephrathah and be famous in Bethlehem. May your house be like the house of Perez, whom Tamar bore to Judah, because of the offspring which the Lord will give you from this young woman" (Ruth 4:11–12). Perez means "breaking forth" (Strong). Something was limited and held back, but now it breaks forth.

Next they spoke of Tamar and Judah, whose history was very shameful. Tamar was Judah's daughter-in-law who dressed up like a harlot and had a child through Judah. If I were Boaz, I would have been insulted if someone likened my fiancée to such a woman. However, this case actually was meant as an encouragement to Boaz, for though Ruth as a Moabitess came from a dark background, so also the birth of Perez came as a breaking forth from a dark background to became a blessing to Israel. Eventually both Perez and the child born of Boaz and Ruth became the means for Jesus Christ to come in the flesh (Matt. 1:3, 5).

The Blessing to Naomi

So Boaz and Ruth were finally married, and they had a son. The women then told Naomi how blessed she was, saying,

"Blessed be the Lord, who has not left you this day without a close relative; and may his name be famous in Israel! And may he be to you a restorer of life and a nourisher of your old age; for your daughter-in-law, who loves you, who is better to you than seven sons, has borne him" (Ruth 4:14–15). This book is called the book of Ruth, but it begins and ends with Naomi. She was no longer Mara (bitter), for now she was truly blessed. Through Boaz, both Naomi and Ruth were blessed. Naomi even gained a restorer of life in her old age. If we follow the Lord, we should never be discouraged. There is always something of the Lord to sustain us. Ruth herself became better to Naomi than seven sons. The Lord would much rather have one such overcomer than seven churchgoers.

The Continuation: Obed, Jesse, and David

In verse 16, Naomi took the child, laid him on her bosom, and became his nurse. Then something interesting happened. It seems it was the neighbors who came into the house who gave this child his name. They named him Obed, which means "serving" or "worshipping" (Easton). It is very meaningful that these two can come together in one person. Obed became the father of Jesse, who was the father of David.

There are three places in the Bible where ten generations are mentioned. The first is in Genesis 5, which goes from Adam to Noah. The second is in Genesis 11, which goes from Shem to Abraham. The third set of ten generations is here in Ruth chapter four. The first set of ten generations covers the experience of redemption, the second covers the experience of God's calling, and this third one covers the experience of being brought from regeneration into the kingdom of God.

I hope we are all impressed with this matter of Christ as our near relative and the natural man, who is inclined to religion, as another even closer relative. Perhaps if we were to see these two—Boaz and the closer kinsman—they might appear nearly identical. How close was Boaz to this other relative? Perhaps very close, so close that it was difficult to tell them apart. What differentiates them in our experience? One desires to take what we have, and the other wants to give Himself to us because He cares about our ultimate profit. May we all give our hearts today to the Lord as Ruth gave herself to Boaz, so that the Lord may fully reveal to us who He is, and expose the one who competes with Him for our heart and mind. May the Lord have mercy on us as we pursue after Him as the unique One that we desire, until He and we are truly joined as one.

Lord, this is our desire!

Works Cited

Brown, Francis, Samuel R. Driver, Charles A. Briggs, and Wilhelm Gesenius. *A Hebrew and English Lexicon of the Old Testament.* London: Oxford University Press, 1939.

Davis, John D. *Dictionary of the Bible.* Nashville: Royal Publishers, Inc., 1973.

Easton, Matthew G. *Illustrated Bible Dictionary.* Thomas Nelson, 1897.

Hitchcock, Roswell D. *New and Complete Analysis of the Holy Bible.* 1869.

Strong, James. *A Concise Dictionary of the Words in the Hebrew Bible.* Madison, NJ, 1890.

Young, Robert. *Analytical Concordance to the Bible.* Grand Rapids: Wm. B. Eerdmans Publishing Co., 1970.

Online Ministry by Titus Chu

MinistryMessages.org is the online archive for the ministry of Titus Chu. This includes audio messages, articles, and books in PDF format, all of which are available as free downloads.

FellowshipJournal.org is an online magazine that features recent sharing by Titus Chu. It also provides brief, daily excerpts from his ministry, as well as news of upcoming events.

"Daily Words for the Christian Life" is an e-letter sent out every Thursday. It features selections from the writings of Titus Chu. To subscribe, visit FellowshipJournal.org/subscribe.

Books by Titus Chu

The books listed below are available in print, Kindle, or iBook format. To purchase them, go to MinistryMessages.org/order. They are also available via Amazon.com and iTunes.

David: After God's Heart

Elijah & Elisha: Living for God's Testimony

Ruth: Growth unto Maturity

Philippians: That I May Gain Christ

A Sketch of Genesis

Two Manners of Life

www.ingramcontent.com/pod-product-compliance
Lightning Source LLC
Chambersburg PA
CBHW031629040426
42452CB00007B/753